What Is Lojban?

.i la lojban. mo

Edited by

Nick Nicholas

John Cowan

What Is Lojban?: .i la lojban. mo
Edited by Nick Nicholas and John Cowan

Published 2003

Publisher's Cataloging-in-Publication
(Provided by Quality Books, Inc.)

What is Lojban?=.i la lojban. mo / edited by Nick Nicholas, John Cowan.
    p.   cm.
Includes index.
LCCN 2003106385
ISBN 0-9660283-1-7

   1. Loglan (Artficial language) I. Nicholas, Nick, 1971- II. Cowan, John Woldemar. III. Title: .i la lojban. mo

PM8590.W43 2003   499'.99
            QBI03-200401

Table of Contents

Organization of this booklet
stura le dei cmacku

This booklet is an introduction to the language Lojban. It is divided into three parts.

Part I gives a general presentation of what the language is, why it exists, and why it should be of interest to you. Part II contains a more formal exposition of the language, consisting of an overview of the language's grammar, a diagrammed summary of its grammar basics, and a discussion of linguistic issues relevant to Lojban. It may be used in conjunction with the introductory lessons available separately. Part III, finally, contains a few texts in Lojban, with parallel translation and glosses, to allow you to get a feel for how the language works.

- The *Introduction* (formerly the *la lojban. mo* brochure) was originally written by Athelstan and Bob LeChevalier in 1988, and updated in 1991 and 2001, incorporating material by Robin Turner.
- The *Overview* was originally written by Bob LeChevalier in 1989, and updated in 1990 (incorporating content by John Cowan) and 2001.
- The *Diagrammed Summary* was originally written by Nora Tansky LeChevalier and Bob LeChevalier in 1990, and updated in 1992 and 2001.
- *Linguistic Issues* is based on material originally contained in the *la lojban. mo* brochure; in *Is Lojban Scientifically Interesting?* originally written by Bob LeChevalier in 1992; and the paper *Loglan and Lojban: A Linguist's Questions And An Amateur's Answers* originally written by John Cowan in 1991, in response to Arnold M. Zwicky's review of James Cooke Brown's 1966 edition of *Loglan 1*. (Zwicky's review was published in *Language* 45:2 (1969), pp. 444–457.)
- The glosses in Part III were made using the program *jbofi'e* by Richard Curnow.
- The cover for the print version was done by Rocket House Studio.

Thanks to Pierre Abbat, Arnt Richard Johansen, Jay Kominek, Jorge Llambías, Steven Lytle, Robin Lee Powell, Adam Raizen, And Rosta, Nora Tansky LeChevalier, Robin Turner, and Scott Weller for their suggestions. For the pronunciation guides, thanks to Alfred Tüting, Philip Netwon, and Jorge Llambías.

Note: This booklet is published by the Logical Language Group, incorporated as a non-profit scientific/educational charity approved by the U.S. Government for tax-deductible donations. We ask that those obtaining our materials by computer register your interest with us by postal or computer mail. We also ask that you consider contributing to The Logical Language Group to help offset our continuing costs in general support of the Lojban community. Contributions can be as small or as great as you like, though we trust that you will find Lojban rewarding enough to contribute a substantial amount. For the current price of this booklet, please check the Lojban website, `http://www.lojban.org`.

.i le dei cmacku cu vasru loi cfari terdjuno datni pe la lojban. .i le cmacku cu se pagbu cida
.i le 1moi pagbu cu naltcila jai jarco ledu'u ly. mo kau kei .e ledu'u ly. zasti mu'i ma kau kei .e ledu'u tu'a ly. cinri do ki'u ma kau .i le 2moi pagbu cu vasru lo ritlymau velski be ly. be'o no'u lo naltcila velski be le gerna sidbo be'o kujoi lo xracartu torvelski be le jicmu gerna be'o kujoi lo prosa be le bauske cuntu poi srana la lojban. .i ka'e pilno le go'i ku joi le cfari ve cilre be fi la lojban. be'o noi ka'e ji'a sepli se cpacu.i le ro 3moi pagbu cu vasru so'u seltcidu pebau la lojban. ge'u .e lo kansa xe fanva .e lo kansa xe vlafanva mu'i lenu do co'a jimpe ledu'u le bangu cu se sazri ta'i ma kau ni'o

- la lidne pagbu po'u le lu la lojban. mo li'u seltcidu pepuku cu krasi se finti la .AT,lstan. joi la lojbab. ca le 1988moi nanca gi'e se ningau ca la 1991moi .e la 2001moi .i ji'a ca la 2001moi co'a vasru loi seltcidu pefi'e la robin.terner.
- .i la naltcila velski cu krasi se finti la lojbab. joi la djan.kau,n. ca la 1989moi nanca gi'e se ningau ca la 1990moi .e la 2001moi
- .i la xracartu torvelski cu krasi se finti la noras.tanskis.lecevalier. joi la lojbab. ca la 1990moi nanca gi'e se ningau ca la 1992moi .e la 2001moi
- .i la bauske se casnu cu se jicmu loi seltcidu poi krasi se vasru le lu la lojban. mo li'u seltcidu ku'o .e la'e lu xu tu'a la lojban. saske cinri li'u noi krasi se finti la lojbab. ca la 1992moi nanca ku'o .e la me la loglan .e la lojban. .i la me la loglan .e la lojban. cu krasi se finti la djan.kau,n. ca

la 1991moi mu'i lenu spuda le pajni prosa befi la .arnold. zuikis. beife la pamoi pe la loglan. ge'u nefi'e la djeimyz.kuk.braun. zi'epede'i la 1966moi .i le la zuikis. pajni prosa cu se gubgau vecu'u le 444moi bi'o 457moi papri be le 45 pi'e 2moi te krefu be le karni po'u la'o gy. Language gy. be'o nede'i la 1969moi

• .i le valsi xe fanva pe le 3moi pagbu cu se cupra sepi'o le mutmi'i po'u la jbofi'e nefi'e la ritcrd.kernous.

• .i le gacri pixra cu se zbasu la'o gy. Rocket House Studio gy.

.i mi ckire la pier.aBAT. .e la .arnt.rikard.iuxansen. goi la tsali ge'u .e la xorxes.jambi,as. .e la djez.KOminek. .e la rabin.lis.pau,el. .e la stivn.laitl. .e la .adam.reizen. .e la .and.rostas. .e la noras.tanskis.lecevalier. .e la robin.terner. .e la skat.uelyr. lenu vo'e cu stidi sidju .i le bacru tadji velciksi te ckire la .alfred.titin. goi la .aulun. ge'u .e la filip.niuton. .e la xorxes.jambi,as.

ni'o ju'ido'u: le dei cmacku cu se gubgau la lojbangirz. noi ba'o flalu binxo lo nalselprali ke saske ja ctuca ke dinterdu'a girzu poi le merko turni cu zanru lenu na cteki le jdini poi se dunda fi le girzu .i mi cpedu lenu le cpacu be lemi datni bei xebe'i le skami cu jungau ly. ledu'u se cinri kei semu'i lenu pelji ja skami mrilu .i ji'a mi cpedu lenu do dunda fi la lojbangirz. mu'i loinu ly pleji fo loinu vrici sarji le lojbo cecmu .i le klani be le jdini poi do dunda cu .e'a jai se jdice do .i ku'i .a'o leni do zanfri la lojban cu banzu lenu do mu'i dunda lo vajni ly. .i ko mu'i lenu do djuno le ca jdima be ledei cukta kei cu tcidu la'e le la lojban. skamrxuebe tcana no'u la'o gy. http://www.lojban.org gy.

I. Introduction

lidne pagbu

Chapter 1. Questions and Answers on Lojban

preti ce'o danfu sera'a la lojban.

1. What is Lojban?

Lojban (/LOZH-bahn/) is a constructed language. Originally called 'Loglan' by project founder Dr. James Cooke Brown, who started the language development in 1955, the goals for the language were first described in the article *Loglan* in *Scientific American*, June 1960. Made well-known by that article and by occasional references in science fiction and computer publications, Loglan/Lojban has been built over four decades by dozens of workers and hundreds of supporters, led since 1987 by The Logical Language Group.

There are many artificial languages, but Loglan/Lojban has been *engineered* to make it unique in several ways. The following are the main features of Lojban:

- Lojban is designed to be used by people in communication with each other, and possibly in the future with computers.
- Lojban is designed to be culturally neutral.
- Lojban grammar is based on the principles of logic.
- Lojban has an unambiguous grammar.
- Lojban has phonetic spelling, and sounds can be divided into words in only one way.
- Lojban is simple compared to natural languages; it is easy to learn.
- Lojban's 1350 root words can be easily combined to form a vocabulary of millions of words.
- Lojban is regular; the rules of the language don't have exceptions.
- Lojban attempts to remove restrictions on creative and clear thought and communication.
- Lojban has a variety of uses, ranging from creative to scientific, from theoretical to practical.

The following sections examine each of these points, while answering the questions most often asked about Lojban.

2. Why was Lojban developed?

Lojban was originally designed to support research on a concept known as the Sapir–Whorf hypothesis. Simply expressed, this hypothesis states that the structure of a language constrains the thinking of people using that language. Lojban allows the full expressive capability of a natural language, but differs in structure from other languages in major ways. This allows it to be used as a test vehicle for scientists studying the relationships between language, thought, and culture. If you are reading this as part of the introductory booklet, further discussion of these issues can be found in the section *Technical Descriptions*.

3. Are there other uses for Lojban?

Yes, several. Due to its unambiguous grammar and simple structure, it also can be easily parsed (broken down for analysis) by computers, making it possible for Lojban to be used in the future for computer–human interaction, and perhaps conversation. Lojban's structure is similar to existing artificial intelligence (AI) programming languages, and it may become be a most powerful adjunct to AI research, especially in the storing and processing of data about the world and people's conceptions of it. There are also linguists interested in Lojban's potential as an intermediate language in computer-aided translation of natural languages; and Lojban is of interest as a potential stepping-stone for students learning other languages. Because Lojban was designed to be culturally neutral, and has a powerful vocabulary easily learned by people of different language origins, some are interested in Lojban's potential as an international language. These are only the beginnings of the Lojban applications that will be developed in the future.

4. Is Lojban a computer language?

Lojban was designed as a *human language*, and not as a computer language. It is therefore intended for use in conversation, reading, writing, and thinking. However, since Lojban can be processed by a computer much more easily than can a natural language, it is only a matter of time before Lojban-based computer applications are developed. Learning and using Lojban doesn't require you to know anything about computers or to talk like one.

5. How is Lojban written? How does it sound?

Lojban uses letters of the Roman alphabet to represent its 6 vowels and 17 consonants. The Lojban character set uses only standard typewriter/computer keyboard keys; capitalization is used rarely, and only to indicate unusual stress in the pronunciation of names. Punctuation is spoken as words. The written language corresponds exactly to the sounds of the spoken language; spelling is phonetic and unambiguous, and the flowing sounds of the language break down into words in only one possible way. These features make computer speech recognition and transcription more practical. Learning to pronounce and spell Lojban is trivial.

Lojban has a smooth, rhythmic sound, somewhat like Italian. However, its consonants create a fullness and power found in Slavic languages like Russian, and the large number of vowel pairs impart a hint of Chinese, Polynesian, and other Oriental languages, though without the tones that make many of those languages difficult for others to learn.

Because there are no idioms to shorten expressions, a Lojban text can be longer than the corresponding colloquial English text. The unambiguous linguistic structures that result are a major benefit that makes this worthwhile; and Lojban has constructions of its own that are rather more succinct than their equivalents in English (such as logic-specific formulations, and expressions of attitude.) Moreover, much of the disambiguating machinery of Lojban is optional; you use them only when you *need* to use them.

As an example of Lojban, Occam's Razor ("The simplest explanation is usually the best") may be translated as:

roda poi velcki cu so'eroi ke ganai saprai gi xagrai
/row-dah poy VELSH-kee shoo so-heh-roy keh GAH-nye
SAHP-rye ghee KHAH-grye/
All somethings which-are explanations mostly-are (if superlatively-simple then superlatively-good).

The apostrophe is pronounced like a short, breathy 'h', and is used to clearly separate the two adjacent vowels for a listener, without requiring a pause between them.

(If you are reading this text in the *What is Lojban?* booklet, a full pronunciation key is available in the *Overview of Lojban Grammar*.)

6. What kind of grammar does Lojban have?

'Grammar' is a word with painful memories for many of us. But though Lojban grammar seems strange at first sight, it is actually quite simple. It is based on a system called predicate logic, which states that in any sentence you have a **relationship** (*selbri* in Lojban) between one or more **arguments** (*sumti*). An argument can be a thing, event, quality or just about anything. To give an example, the English sentence

Chris adores Pat

has a relation *adore*, between two arguments, *Chris* and *Pat*. In Lojban this would be

la kris. prami la pat.

or, if you prefer,

la kris. la pat. prami

(The full stops mean that you have to pause slightly to separate the words—
anythingelseinLojbancanberuntogetherwithoutbeingmisunderstood).

You might be thinking "Well in that case a relationship is a verb and an argument is a noun, so why bother with special terminology like *selbri* and whatnot?" However, in Lojban Chris's feelings about Pat might be described like this:

la pat. melbi
Pat is beautiful.

In English you have a verb ('doing word'), *is*, and an adjective ('describing word'), *beautiful*. In Turkish, you would say *Pat güzel*, which is a noun and an adjective, with no verb required. In Chinese you would use *meili*, a 'stative verb' — but enough! In Lojban you don't need all these language-specific notions.

Now, if there are no nouns, verbs, subjects or objects in Lojban, how do we know that la kris. la pat. prami means that Chris adores Pat and not the other way? Different languages handle this problem differently. In English it is done with word order, and when that isn't enough, with prepositions (words like *at, from, to, with* and so on). In other languages, like Latin or Turkish, it's done by changing the form of the words, e.g. *Pat'i Chris sever* in Turkish means "Chris loves Pat", not "Pat loves Chris."

In Lojban, the order in which arguments appear is built in to the meaning of the word. For example, the word dunda means *give*, but its full meaning is:

$$x_1 \text{ gives } x_2 \text{ to } x_3$$

So mi pu dunda le cukta le ninmu means "I gave the book to the woman", not "I gave the woman to the book").

The important point is that Lojban has a lot of what we would call 'grammar', but nearly all of this is contained in the *cmavo* (structure words), and you can use as many or as few of them as you want.

7. What else is distinctive about Lojban grammar?
In Lojban, it is equally easy to speak of something as being an action as it is to speak of it as being a state of existence. The distinction between the two can be ignored, or can be explicitly expressed in a variety of ways:

• by associating concepts in *tanru* metaphors (combinations of *selbri* into single expressions giving novel meanings), involving words like gasnu ('do'), zasti ('exist'), zukte ('act with purpose');

- with a variety of 'operators' (*cmavo*) dealing with abstractions such as events, states, properties, amounts, ideas, experience, and truth;
- or with four pre-defined varieties of causality (others can be developed through *tanru* metaphor).

A major benefit of using a predicate grammar is that Lojban doesn't have inflections and declensions on nouns, verbs, and adjectives. Most natural languages have evolved such variations to reduce ambiguity as to how words are related in a sentence. Language change has made these inflections and declensions highly irregular and thus difficult to learn. Lojban uses the simple but flexible predicate relationship to erase both the irregularity and the declensions.

Tense and location markers (inflections), adverbs, and prepositions are combined into one part of speech. New preposition-like forms can be built at will from predicates; these allow the user to expand upon a sentence by attaching and relating arguments not normally included in the meaning of a word.

Numbers and quantifiers are conceptually expanded from natural languages. *Many, enough, too much, a few,* and *at least* are among concepts that are expressed as numbers in Lojban. Thus "it costs $3.95" and "it costs too much" are grammatically identical, and one can talk of being "enough-th in line" for tickets to a sellout movie. Core concepts of logic, mathematics, and science are built into the root vocabulary. They enhance discussion of those topics, and are surprisingly useful in ordinary speech, too.

Predicate logic can express a wide variety of human thought; Lojban also has non-logical constructs that do not affect or obscure the logical structure, allowing communications that are not amenable to logical analysis. For example, Lojban has a full set of emotional indicators, which are similar to such interjections in English as *Oh!*, *Aha!*, and *Wheee!*, but each has a specific meaning. Similarly, Lojban has indicators of the speaker's relationship to what is said (whether it is hearsay, direct observation, logical deduction, etc.) similar to those found in some Native American languages.

Lojban supports metalinguistic discussion about the sentences being spoken while remaining unambiguous. Lojban also supports a variety of 'tense' logic that allows one to be extremely specific about time and space (and space–time) relationships. A substantial portion of Lojban's grammar is designed to support unambiguous statement of mathematical expressions and relations in a manner compatible both with international usage and the rest of Lojban's grammar.

Lojban 'parts of speech' are convertible from one to another by using short structure words (called *cmavo*). One can make numbers serve as nouns or verbs, or invent new numbers and prepositions. Lojban removes many of the constraints on human thought, while preserving tight control on structural syntax.

8. Lojban seems complex. How hard is it to learn?

Lojban is actually much simpler than natural languages. It is only slightly more complex in its grammar than the current generation of computer languages (such as C++ and Perl). Lojban seems complex only because the varieties of human thought are complex, and Lojban is designed to minimize constraints on those thoughts. Lojban text can appear longer and more complex due to its lack of idiom, its complete explicitness of logical structure, and most importantly, its unfamiliarity. On the other hand, conversational speech uses less than half of the possible grammatical structures, leaving the rest for writing and for other circumstances when one is likely to take time to carefully formulate exact logical phrasings.

Lojban's pronunciation, spelling, word formation, and grammar rules are fixed, and the language is free of exceptions to these rules. Such exceptions are the bane of learning to speak a natural language *correctly*. Without the burden of ambiguity, Lojban users can be precise and specific more easily than in other languages.

Because Lojban's grammar is simple, it is easier to learn than other languages. Using flashcard-like techniques, a working vocabulary including the complete set of 1350 root words can take 8–12 weeks of study at 1 hour per day. It is by no means uncommon for people who embark on learning Lojban to be able to write grammatical Lojban within a few days, and to hold at least a limited conversation within a few weeks. Natural languages, especially English, take several years to learn to a comparable level of skill.

The available Lojban teaching materials are so structured that you can learn the language without classroom instruction or a close community of speakers. Communication practice with others is needed to achieve fluency, but you can start using the language as you achieve proficiency.

9. What do you mean by 'unambiguous'?

Lojban has an unambiguous grammar (proven by computer analysis of a formal grammar), pronunciation, and **morphology** (word forms). In practice this means that the person who reads or hears a Lojban sentence is never in doubt as to what words it contains or what roles they play in the sentence. This is true even if the words are unfamiliar, so long as the spelling and grammar rules are known. Lojban has no words that sound alike but have different meanings (like *herd* and *heard*), that have multiple unrelated meanings (*set*), or that differ only in punctuation but not in sound (like the abominable *its* and *it's*). There is never any doubt about where words begin and end (if you hear *cargo ship*, do you hear two words or three?) Most important, the function of each word is inescapably clear; there is nothing like the English sentence *Time flies like an arrow*, in which any of the first three words could be the verb.

Lojban is *not* entirely unambiguous, of course; human beings occasionally desire to be ambiguous in their expressions. In Lojban, this ambiguity is limited to semantics, *tanru* metaphor, and intentional omission of information (ellipsis).

Semantic ambiguity results because words in natural languages represent families of concepts rather than individual meanings. These meanings often have only weak semantic relationships to each other (the English word *run* is a good example.) In addition, each individual's personal experiences provide emotional connotations to words. By providing a fresh, culturally-neutral start, Lojban attempts to minimize the transference of these associations as people learn the language. Most Lojban words do not much resemble corresponding words in other languages; the differences aid in making this fresh start possible.

Lojban's powerful *tanru* (combinations of *selbri* into novel concepts) and word-building features make it easy to make fine distinctions between concepts. This discourages the tendency for individual words to acquire families of meanings. Lojban's *tanru* metaphors are themselves ambiguous; they specify a relationship between concepts, but not what the relationship is. That relationship can be made explicit using unambiguous logical constructs if necessary, or can be left vague, as the speaker typically desires. Similarly, portions of the logical structure of a Lojban expression can be omitted, greatly simplifying the expression while causing some ambiguity. Unlike in the natural languages, though, this ambiguity is readily identified by a reader or listener. Thus all ambiguity in Lojban is constrained and recognizable, and can be clarified as necessary by further interaction.

This precision in no way confines the meaning of a Lojban sentence. It is possible to be fanciful or ridiculous, to tell lies, or to be misunderstood. You can be very specific, or you can be intentionally vague. Your hearer may not understand what you *meant*, but will always understand what you *said*.

10. Can you make jokes in an unambiguous language?

Most humor arises from situation and character and is as funny in Lojban as in any language. Humor based on word play, of course, is language-dependent. Lojban has no homonyms, and hence no simple puns; puns derived from similar sounds are still possible, and have in fact been attempted (for example in the Lojban translation of *Alice in Wonderland*). Since Lojban will almost always be a second language, bilingual puns and word play abound, often based on the relative ambiguity of the other languages involved. Humor based on internal grammatical ambiguity is of course impossible in Lojban, but humor based on nonsensical statements, or on logical structures that would be difficult to clearly express in another language, becomes easier.

As speakers become fluent, and conventional phrases come into use, Lojban will develop its own forms of spoonerisms and subtle puns. Unique forms of Lojban word-play have already turned up; they exploit the way small variations in Lojban grammar create unexpected variations in meaning, and the capability to simply express rather mind-boggling relationships. Like all word-play, these lose zest when translated into other languages.

Related to humor is the aphorism: the pithy saying that gains pungency or poignancy from terse, elegant phrasing. Lojban seems as capable of aphorisms as any language, perhaps more than most; however, because the language is so young, few such aphorisms have been devised to date.

11. Isn't Esperanto the 'international language'?

There have been hundreds of artificial international languages developed, of which Esperanto is the most successful and widely known. Esperanto, like most other such languages, was based on European languages in both grammar and vocabulary. Although it manages to be relatively neutral between them, it still retains an inherent cultural bias which makes it unsuited for most of the purposes that Lojban was designed for.

Lojban is culturally fully neutral. Its vocabulary was built algorithmically using today's six most widely spoken languages: Chinese, Hindi, English, Russian, Spanish, and Arabic. Lojban's words thus show roots in three major families of languages spoken by most of the world's people. Lojban's grammar accommodates structures found in non-European languages, and uses sounds found in many of the world's languages. Coupled with the potential computer applications that will make Lojban a useful language to know, Lojban's potential as an international language may be more far-reaching than Esperanto's.

Lojban was not designed primarily to be an international language, however, but rather as a linguistic tool for studying and understanding language. Its linguistic and computer applications make Lojban unique among proposed international languages: Lojban can be successful without immediately being accepted and adopted everywhere, and Lojban can be useful and interesting even to those skeptical of or hostile towards the international language movement.

Since Lojban is also not in direct competition with Esperanto, it has proven attractive to Esperantists interested in acquiring a new perspective on their own international language, and who feel less threatened because Lojban has different goals. Lojban's supporters recognize that it will take decades for Lojban to acquire both the number and variety of speakers and the extensive history of usage that marks Esperanto culture. Meanwhile, each language community has much to learn from the other; this process is already well underway.

12. How about English as an international language?
English is commonly used as an 'international language' in the fields of science and technology, and is probably the most widely spoken language in the world. American dominance of technology in the twentieth century has caused massive borrowing from English into other languages that do not have words for all these new concepts. This dominance, and a heritage of colonialism and imperialism that has built resentment towards American and European impositions on native cultures, has caused recent movements in other countries *away* from English. The rising influence of other non–English-speaking countries on world economics, science, and technology makes further declines in the universality of English likely.

In addition, many who know English as a second language speak it only minimally, though they may be able to read or understand many words. India is a prominent example of a country where English is the only language more or less understood throughout the country, which has about 1500 languages and dialects; but the English spoken in India is often unintelligible to Americans or Britons. In fact, English is one of the most difficult languages to learn to use well. In countries where English is spoken along with other languages, it has been adapted into dialects which match the local culture and borrow words from the other local languages. Some of these dialects are as much as 70% unintelligible to American or British speakers, or to each other. As such, there is no single English language to call an 'international' one.

Lojban is a single language, with design features to discourage breaking up into separate languages. While it was developed primarily by Americans, and was designed to be at least as expressive as English is, Lojban's cultural neutrality gives equal priority to the structures and concepts of other languages and cultures. This cultural neutrality enhances Lojban's acceptability as an international language. Since it is as capable as English is of generating or borrowing any words needed to support the concepts of science and technology, and has special advantages for computer applications, Lojban is likely to spread worldwide through the technological community. Far more so than English, Lojban is simple and easy to learn for people of all cultures.

13. Can poetry be written in a 'logical' language or an 'unambiguous' one?

Original poetry has already been written in Lojban, and some has been translated into the language. Lojban's powerful *tanru* metaphor structure allows you to build concepts into words easily, as you need them, and has been used to create colorful images and to convey moving emotions. A Lojban speaker doesn't need a dictionary to use and understand millions of words that can potentially exist in the language. The absence of cultural constraints makes consideration of new ideas and relationships easier than in natural languages, spurring creativity. Lojban aids in communicating abstractions by identifying their nature explicitly. Lojban is thus a very powerful language, not only for poetry, but for discussing such abstract fields as philosophy, physics, metaphysics, and religion.

Lojban poets are already experimenting with new (and old) forms of poetry that seem especially well suited to the rhythm, sound, and flow of the language. Rarely do poets have such an opportunity to affect the development of a new language as they now can with Lojban. Lojban's rich and powerful. Lojban unleashes the full potential of poetic expression to communicate both concrete and abstract ideas.

14. How was Lojban developed?

The language, then called 'Loglan', was first described in the 1950s by Dr. James Cooke Brown. The 1960 Scientific American article *Loglan* was his call for assistance in developing the language. A revolution in linguistics was simultaneously taking place, resulting in a rapidly increasing knowledge of the nature of human language; this changed the requirements for the developing language. The first widely distributed Loglan dictionary and language description did not

appear until 1975; the incompleteness of this description and con-
tinued development work discouraged people from learning the
language. Furthermore, computers caught up with Loglan just then,
making it possible to refine the grammar, eliminate ambiguity and
mathematically prove its absence. For over forty years, this work has
been performed by volunteers, and without financial support. Now,
after several versions of the language, people have been learning and
using the current version, which is the first to be called 'Lojban' (from
the roots "logical-language" in Lojban).

This version is the first version with a stable vocabulary, and the
first to have a stable and completely defined grammar. The stabiliza-
tion of the language in this version has followed a painstaking and
extensive period of research and analysis, between 1988 and 1998.
Thus, in an important sense, Lojban is a very new language. To ensure
Lojban remains stable while people learn it, the language definition is
being closely controlled; the grammar and core vocabulary have
already been baselined (frozen) for several years. When the number of
speakers has grown significantly, and a Lojban literature has developed, Lojban will be treated like a natural language and allowed to
grow and flourish without constraint, as do other natural languages.

15. How many people speak Lojban?

Questions of how many people speak a language greatly depend on
your presuppositions and definitions—which a language like Lojban,
at least, can make explicit! The on-line Lojban mailing list, which
constitutes the largest community of people using the language, has
over 200 subscribers, with well over 20 regular posters as of this
writing. The level of confidence of the language community has
already risen to such a level that there is a Lojban-language–only
discussion group, as well as the general mailing list. Lojban has also
been used extensively in real-time conversation, both electronically
(IRC) and face-to-face. Though the Lojban-speaking community is so
widely diffused that the opportunity for conversation does not arise
frequently, the number of Lojbanists who can sustain a conversation
in the language certainly ranges beyond what can be counted on the
fingers of one hand, and is steadily increasing. Lojban has been

proven in communicative use for well over a decade, and the range and expressivity of the language is being continually explored by the language community.

The first speakers of Lojban have a unique opportunity. They are the history-makers who will shape the flavor of the first totally new language to achieve broad speakability. Their ideas will be most influential in setting the patterns of usage that others will learn from. Their experiences will teach things about language that have never before been learned — or learnable.

16. Why should I learn Lojban?

There are several reasons for learning the language now. Those who are working with the language now are actively consulted for their opinions on how to teach and spread the language. Within a few weeks of work learning from the materials already written, you will be able to work with those who have already started. You will be a significant part of this small but rapidly growing community. You will receive personal attention to any problems you have with the language from those leading the effort. If you are truly ambitious and committed to the language, you are welcome to join in that leadership.

Those with a computer background who learn the language now will be the leaders in developing the earliest practical computer applications for the language. Meanwhile, computer-oriented Lojbanists can also aid in developing computer-aided instruction tools or converting existing software to run on new computers.

People not interested in computers will also find Lojban a valuable language. You may be interested in the Sapir–Whorf hypothesis, and in the scientific tests to be planned and conducted, or in other language-related research. You may be interested in Lojban's potential as an international language, and in the attempts to use the language to reach across cultural boundaries.

Regardless of your background, you will find learning Lojban to be a mind-expanding experience. Learning any language other than your native tongue broadens your perspectives and allows you to transcend the necessarily limited viewpoints of your native language's culture. Lojban, being simpler to learn than natural languages, provides this benefit much more quickly than does the study of other languages. And being quite different from natural languages, Lojban provides this benefit more directly.

Having learned Lojban, you will find it easier to learn other languages and to communicate with people from other backgrounds, regardless of the language studied; the linguistic principles you learn while learning Lojban are applicable to these languages and the communication problems they entail. The logical organization embedded in Lojban will aid you in organizing and clarifying your thoughts. Your new perspective on language, ambiguity, and communication will allow you to express those thoughts more clearly, even when you use an ambiguous natural language.

You needn't learn Lojban for any practical purpose, however. Many, if not most, of those who are learning Lojban are doing so because it is fun. Learning Lojban is intellectually stimulating, providing human interaction (a way to meet other people and get to know them) and mental challenge. Lojban has all the benefits of games designed for entertainment, with the side benefit of that entertainment developing into a useful skill.

Learning Lojban as an intellectual toy means that you can get enjoyment from learning Lojban without anywhere near the effort needed to benefit from studying other languages. While becoming fluent in Lojban will probably take hundreds of hours over several months, you can feel some sense of accomplishment in the language after just a couple of hours of study. You can use Lojban immediately for fun, while gaining skill with greater experience.

17. How do I learn Lojban?

This text appears in a booklet including a description of the grammar of Lojban and some introductory learning materials. If you are reading this text in a separately printed brochure, you may write to the Logical Language Group at the address found at the end of this brochure, and we will be happy to provide the complete booklet. We request a contribution of $5 to cover its cost.

If you are reading this brochure on-line, or have access to the Internet, the complete *What is Lojban?* booklet is also available on the World Wide Web for free at the address:

```
http://www.lojban.org/publications/level0.html
```

Once you have read this booklet, there are several directions you may proceed, depending on your goals for use of the language.

Most people learning the language will work for some time on their own before working with others. We recommend, where possible, that you identify at least one other person to study and interact with, either in person or by mail. The Logical Language Group maintains lists of Lojban students of various degrees of skill and activity levels. There is also both a general and an in-Lojban discussion group available on the Internet. Information will be found at the end of this document.

Almost any use you wish to make of Lojban requires some degree of mastery of the basic vocabulary. You can learn enough Lojban grammar to support conversation in just a couple of hours, but you will need vocabulary in order to use that grammar.

You can learn the Lojban vocabulary using computer software. The Logical Language Group has computer-aided–teaching programs distributed under the name *LogFlash*, with MS-DOS/Windows, Macintosh and Unix versions currently available. The software is based on flash-card teaching techniques, which are extremely efficient in helping you learn the vocabulary. Other computer software is available, including a parser and a glosser.

You can learn the Lojban grammar in several ways, including by studying the examples in our on-line text archives and mailing lists, and by going through the formal grammar description. (The formal grammars are available in two formats, *YACC* and simplified *E-BNF*.)

An introduction to the grammar of Lojban will be found in *Technical Descriptions* in the *What is Lojban?* booklet. There is also a set of introductory lessons available (these cover the basics of the language, but at a more leisurely pace): *Lojban for Beginners*, by Robin Turner and Nick Nicholas. A complete grammatical description of Lojban, *The*

Complete Lojban Language by John W. Cowan, was published by the Logical Language Group in 1997. This is an authoritative reference, and can be used as an aid to learning the advanced features of the language.

A formal Lojban dictionary is being compiled, and will encompass the word lists already available from the Logical Language Group as of this writing. Draft versions of the dictionary are available on the Lojban web site (see contact details below).

Of course the only way to really learn a language is to *use* it. The Logical Language Group will assist you in finding other Lojban students of comparable skill level and interests, either in your local area or reachable by post or electronic mail. The on-line Lojban discussion groups regularly contain Lojban text, some with detailed translations and some without translation, as well as discussions of language points by various members of the Lojban community. There is also a discussion group specifically for beginners as of this writing. Of course the best way to use the language is to recruit friends and associates into studying and using the language with you. Even if they are not interested in the same language goals as you are, the 'hobbyist' aspect of the language will provide interesting and stimulating entertainment for all concerned.

18. What is The Logical Language Group?

The Logical Language Group, Inc. is a non-profit organization, the embodiment of the Loglan/Lojban community. We were founded to complete the language development process, to develop and publish teaching materials, to organize and teach the community, to promote applications of Lojban, and to initiate and lead research efforts in linguistics, language education, and other areas related to Lojban. Simply put, our purpose is to serve you in all manner of things Lojbanic. The Logical Language Group is not affiliated with The Loglan Institute, Inc., the organization founded by James Cooke Brown.

The Logical Language Group is also called la lojbangirz. (*/lah lozh-BAHN-geerz./*), its Lojban name. It was founded informally in 1987, and incorporated in 1988. The U.S. Internal Revenue Service approved our status as a non-profit educational/scientific charity in 1989, making donations and grants to the organization deductible under U.S. tax law.

Loglan/Lojban has been developed almost totally by volunteer labor and small donations of money. Lojban attracts people who are willing to devote a lot of time and effort to seeing their dreams become reality. Thus, our only income has been money derived from sales of our publications, and donations from interested supporters.

The Logical Language Group publishes and sells printed materials on Lojban. All language definition information is considered in the public domain, and most Logical Language Group publications are distributed under a policy which allows not-for-charge copying and redistribution. Computer versions of many of our publications are available on-line at no charge. We ask people who receive our materials by any of these means to let us know, so that we may better serve you, and donate liberally, so that we may continue to serve you.

Most materials that we sell require either prior payment, an informal commitment to pay on your part, or your statement that you cannot afford to pay for materials (in which case our supplying these materials is at our discretion). We attempt to flexibly support Lojbanists who have financial constraints, and will accept reasonable offers of reduced or delayed payments subject to our financial condition, given your commitment to actively maintain contact and involvement with the community. Obviously, the level of your prior and current activity and any commitments you make to learning the language, or to volunteer work for la lojbangirz., will be factored into our decision.

la lojbangirz. has a special commitment to support Lojbanists outside the U.S., because so many of the language goals are dependent on building an international community of speakers, and because we recognize the difficulties caused by the international currency market and the relative wealth of nations. We can accept bank cheques in most currencies and international payment via PayPal. We also encourage people to form groups so that they can receive a single copy of our materials, copying or passing them to others to keep the per-person costs low. We expect a lower standard of contact and contribution from overseas Lojbanists when deciding whether to continue sending our materials at reduced or no charge.

We ask all recipients of our materials to help us financially in any way you can. The Logical Language Group needs your gifts for support of the Loglan/Lojban project. Artificial languages are historically not self-sustaining financially, and have difficulty receiving outside support. The Logical Language Group, Inc. is prohibited by its bylaws from spending more than 15% of its expenses for administrative purposes, except by special agreement with a donor who agrees to cover such added costs in full.

19. How does The Logical Language Group serve the community?
The Logical Language Group coordinates and promotes activities involving Lojban and the Lojban community. In that role, it publishes materials enabling people to learn the language, and facilitates their forming a community of speakers. Most people involved with Lojban stay informed by checking our web page or participating in the Lojban mailing lists (see contact details below). The Logical Language Group also publishes newsletters and journals, including both general news, aimed at those not actively involved in learning and using the language, and more specific material, including discussions of features of the language, debates on research issues and applications, letters from the community and responses, and Lojban writings and translations.

Our printed publications are free of advertisements (other than our own ordering information, and occasional mention of individuals and organizations who have contributed particular service to our efforts); and we do not sell our mailing list. Our publications are distributed as cheaply as possible to encourage new people to participate. In the interest of attracting the widest audience possible, we are committed to distributing as much material as possible using the 'open source' concept for computer software and a similar policy for printed publications. This policy retains our copyrights but allows you, with relatively few restrictions, to copy our materials for your friends.

Certain materials that we publish contain information that we place in the public domain. **All language definition information is considered to be public.**

If you are attempting to learn the language, we will provide as much help as we can to assist you. We will put you in touch with Lojbanists who might be interested in studying or communicating with you in the language. You can also send your writings to us for review, or for indirect exchange with others. We try to foster research and social interaction among those who are learning, or who have already learned the language. We aid such people in organizing, leading, and teaching formal classes and study groups, and will sponsor affiliated groups in local areas where non-profit sponsorship can be of benefit. We conduct an annual celebration of the language and community (July or August), called 'Logfest', in conjunction with our annual business meeting in the Washington DC area. We also expect to support other local meetings and gatherings as the community grows.

Of course, we also try to publicize the language. Our representatives can attend meetings to give presentations on the language. We distribute informational material, including these booklets. Through our efforts, and with your help, the community of Lojbanists is rapidly growing.

20. What can I do now?

You can become involved in the Lojban project in a variety of ways, depending on your background and interests, and on your available time:

- you can participate in completing the language documentation;
- you can devise applications for Lojban in computers, education, linguistics, and other fields;
- you can help in organizing Lojbanists in your area, and in recruiting new Lojbanists;
- you can help in teaching the language to new people (even while learning yourself);
- you can assist in spreading Lojban to non–English-speaking cultures by helping translate materials into other languages, and by identifying, recruiting, and communicating with contacts in other

countries (international involvement is vital to ensuring that Lojban remains culturally neutral);

- you can contribute financially to support our organization, its activities, and its publications;
- you can use Lojban in composition, translation, and conversation with other Lojbanists.

For many of these activities, you need to learn the language first. However, even those who haven't yet had time to learn the language can assist in recruiting and contributing ideas to the effort.

Helping to publicize the language, of course, does not take a lot of time, or necessarily even knowing the language. Talk to friends, relatives and colleagues. We will gladly provide copies of this brochure on request. Lojban tends to sell itself; people who learn of it are more often than not intrigued by it.

Keep in touch with us. We want to know your ideas and opinions on the language, on our various activities, and on our products. We welcome open debate on the language, and have even printed and made available writings that are critical of various aspects of our efforts, when they are of sufficient general interest. Open debate aids in understanding and improves the overall quality of the language and of our presentation of it to the world. Much of the language design is now complete, and the Logical Language Group is committed to maintaining a stable version of the language. Nonetheless, we would rather hear criticism now within our community and either correct our problems or prepare an adequate response, than do so later when such issues are raised by outsiders.

In short, Lojban is a product of *all* of the community, including *you* — if you choose.

Of course, the most important thing you can do is:

> **Use Lojban!:** Lojban will not really achieve the status of 'language' until people *use* it. We need creative people to write Lojban prose, poetry, and dialog. We need translations made from fiction, technical literature, from religious and philosophical writings, and from music. *Only* in this way will Lojban be proven practical, and gain the credibility it needs to succeed.

21. Who do I contact?

We have several volunteers who serve to coordinate Lojban activities in specific regions of the world. There is also a limited amount of Lojban materials translated into languages other than English. This support is constantly being added to; please contact us for details.

The Logical Language Group's website, which contains all its publicly available information, is at:

        http://www.lojban.org

Several active Lojban-related mailing lists are available on the Internet. The general Lojban list is `lojban`; the list for discussions in Lojban only is `jbosnu`; and the list specifically for beginners is `lojban-beginners`. They may be accessed as follows:

Web	• `http://groups.yahoo.com/group/lojban`
	• `http://groups.yahoo.com/group/jbosnu`
	• `http://www.lojban.org/lsg2/` (lojban-beginners)
Email	• `lojban@yahoogroups.com`
	• `jbosnu@yahoogroups.com`
	• `lojban-beginners@chain.digitalkingdom.org`
Subscribe	`http://www.lojban.org/lsg2/` for all lists.

(All lists are mirrored outside `yahoo.com`, on the Lojban web server: `http://www.lojban.org/lsg2/`)

If you have received a registration form and an order form with this booklet, you can provide us with useful information to aid us in serving you, and can order some of our materials. Write or call:

The Logical Language Group, Inc.
2904 Beau Lane
Fairfax, VA 22031
U.S.A.
(+1 703) 385-0273
E-mail can be sent to us at: `lojban@lojban.org`

.e'osai ko sarji la lojban.
/eh-ho-sigh, ko-SAHR-zhee, lah LOZH-bahn./
Please support Lojban!

II. Technical Descriptions

certu velskicu

Chapter 2. Overview of Lojban Grammar

naltcila velski be le lojbo gerna sidbo

This overview of Lojban will hopefully give you a good feel for the design and scope of the language. It serves as an introduction to learning the language; most of the special terminology used elsewhere is defined here. This overview is *not* complete, nor detailed; much is glossed over. To actually learn the language you must study the available reference or teaching materials.

The material following is divided up into the major facets of language description. These are:

Orthography
   the way the language is written

Phonology
   the way the language sounds

Morphology
   the structure of words

Semantics
   the meanings of words, sentences, and expressions

Grammar
   the ways in which words may be put together

For many special terms, we will give a definition, and then the Lojban word for the concept. The Lojban words are then used, to avoid confusion due to the various meanings of the English jargon words. The Lojban words are also what is used in other publications about the language.

Orthography

Lojban uses the Roman alphabet, consisting of the following letters and symbols:

’ , . a b c d e f g i j k l m n o p r s t u v x y z

omitting the letters *h*, *q*, and *w*. The three special characters are *not* punctuation:

- The apostrophe represents a specific sound, similar to the English /h/.
- The period is an optional reminder to the reader, representing a mandatory pause dictated by the rules of the language. Such pauses can be of any duration, and are part of the **morphology**, or word formation rules, and not the grammar.
- The comma is used to indicate a syllable break within a word, generally one that is not obvious to the reader.

The alphabet order given above is that of the ASCII symbol set, most widely used in computers for sorting and searching.

Lojban does not require capitalization of any word type, including proper names, and such capitalization is discouraged. Capital letters are used instead to indicate non-standard stress in pronunciation of Lojbanized names. Thus the English name *Josephine*, as normally pronounced, is Lojbanized as DJOsefin, pronounced /JO,seh,feen/. Without the capitalization, Lojban stress rules would force the /seh/ syllable to be stressed.

Lojban's alphabet and pronunciation rules bring about what is called **audio-visual isomorphism**. There is not only a unique symbol to represent each sound of Lojban, but also a single correct way to separate the sounds of continuous Lojban speech into words. Similarly, a Lojban text may be read off sound by sound, using pronunciation and stress rules, to form an unambiguous uttered expression. Spelling in Lojban is thus trivial to learn.

Phonology

Each Lojban sound is uniquely assigned to a single letter, or combination of letters. Each letter is defined to have a particular set of possible pronunciations, such that there is no overlap between letter sounds.

Most of the consonants are pronounced exactly as they are most commonly pronounced in English. The following gives English and Lojban examples for these.

> **Note:** In the following examples, the English word and the Lojban word are the same where possible. (This was not possible for j.)

Unvoiced

p	/p/	*powder*	purmo	/POOR,mo/
f	/f/	*fall*	farlu	/FAHR,loo/
t	/t/	*time*	temci	/TEM,shee/
s	/s/	*soldier*	sonci	/SONE,shee/
k	/k/	*keen*	kinli	/KEEN,lee/

Voiced

b	/b/	*bottle*	botpi	/BOAT,pee/
v	/v/	*voice*	voksa	/VOAK,sah/
d	/d/	*dance*	dansu	/DAHN,soo/
z	/z/	*zinc*	zinki	/ZEEN,kee/
g	/g/	*goose*	gunse	/GOON,seh/

Incidentally, for these examples, the Lojban example is a close equivalent of the English example used, showing that some words in Lojban are very similar to their English counterparts. In the pronunciation guides, note the conventions of capitalizing stressed syllables and of separating syllables with commas. These conventions could optionally be used in the Lojban words themselves, but are not necessary.

In the above examples, the consonants in the first table are called **unvoiced consonants**, because they are spoken without voicing them using the vocal folds. The consonants in the second table are their **voiced** equivalents.

When a consonant is made by touching the tongue so as to block air passage, it is called a **stop** (p, b, t, d, k, g). If the blockage is incomplete, and air rubs between the tongue and the roof of the mouth, it is called a **fricative** (f, v, s, z). For example, k is an unvoiced stop in the back of the mouth. Its unvoiced fricative equivalent is x, which is rarely found in English (the Scottish *loch*, as in *Loch Ness monster*, is an example).

x	/kh/	*loch*	lalxu	/LAHL,khoo/
	—		xriso	/KHREE,so/

Two other fricatives are c and j. c is the unvoiced /sh/ sound that is usually represented by two letters in English. j is its voiced equivalent, rarely occurring alone in English (but see below).

c	/sh/	*shirt*	creka	/SHREH,kah/
		English	glico	/GLEE,sho/
j	/zh/	*measure*	lojban	/LOZH,bahn/
		azure		

These two fricatives occur frequently in English combined with a stop (giving **affricates**). Lojban phonology recognizes this, and the /ch/ sound is written tc, while the /j/ sound is written dj.

tc	/tsh/ = /ch/	*much*	mutce	/MU,cheh/
dj	/dzh/ = /j/	*jaw*	xedja	/KHED,jah/

The other four Lojban consonants are also pronounced as in English. But each has two possible pronunciations. The normal Lojban pronunciation is shown in the first table. In names, borrowings, and a few other situations, however, these consonants can occur in a syllable of their own, with no vowel. In this case they are called **syllabic consonants**, and are pronounced as in the second table.

Non-syllabic

l	/l/	*late*	lerci	/LEHR,shee/
m	/m/	*move*	muvdu	/MOVE,du/
n	/n/	*nose*	nazbi	/NAHZ,bee/
r	/r/	*rock*	rokci	/ROKE,shee/

Syllabic

l	/l/	*bottle*		
		Carl	kar,l	/KAHR,l/
m	/m/	*bottom*		
		Miriam	miri,m	/MEE,ree,m/
n	/n/	*button*		
		Ellen	el,n	/EHL,n/
r	/r/	*letter*		
		Burt	brt	/brt/

Note: The names given above have syllabic consonants in American English. In British English, *Burt* is pronounced instead as byt, *Carl* as kal, *Ellen* usually as .elyn or .elen, and *Miriam* as miri,ym.

Consonants may be found in pairs, or even in triples, in many Lojban words; even longer clusters of consonants, often including at least one syllabic consonant, may be found in Lojbanized names or borrowings. Some of these clusters may appear strange to the English speaker (for example mlatu /MLAH,tu/), but all permitted clusters were chosen so as to be quite pronounceable by most speakers and understandable to most listeners. If you run across a cluster that you simply cannot pronounce because of its unfamiliarity, it is permissible to insert a very short *non-Lojban* vowel sound between them. The English /i/ as in *bit* is recommended for English speakers.

The basic Lojban vowels are best described as being similar to the vowels of Spanish and Italian. These languages use pure vowels, whereas English commonly uses vowels that are complexes of two or more pure vowels called **diphthongs** (2-sounds) or **triphthongs** (3-sounds). English speakers must work at keeping the sounds pure; a crisp, clipped speech tends to help, along with keeping the lips and tongue tensed (for example by smiling tightly) while speaking.

There are five common vowels (a, e, i, o, u), and one special-purpose vowel (y). English words that are close in pronunciation are given, but few speakers pronounce these words in English with the purity and tension needed in Lojban pronunciation.

a	/ah/	*father*, (American) *top*	patfu	/PAHT,foo/
e	/eh/	*bet, lens*	lenjo	/LENN,zho/
i	/ee/	*green, machine*	minji	/MEEN,zhee/
o	/o/	*joke, note*	notci	/NO,chee/
u	/u/	*boot, shoe*	cutci	/SHOE,chee/
y	/uh/	*sofa, above*	lobypli	/LOBE,uh,plee/

The sound represented by y, called 'schwa', is a totally relaxed sound, contrasting with all the other tensed vowels. So the Lojban vowels are maximally separated among possible vowel sounds. English speakers must be especially careful to ensure that a final unstressed vowel a in a Lojban word is kept tensed, and not relaxed as in the English *sofa* (compare the equivalent Lojban sfofa /SFO,fah/, not sfofy /SFO,fuh/).

Lojban has diphthongs as well, but these are always represented by the two vowels that combine to form them:

Rising diphthongs

ai	/ai/	*high*	bai	*bye*
au	/au/	*cow*	vau	*vow*
ei	/ei/	*bay*	pei	*pay*
oi	/oi/	*boy*	coi	*shoy*

Falling diphthongs

ia	/yah/	*yard*	ua	/wah/	*wander*
ie	/yeh/	*yell*	ue	/weh/	*well*
ii	/yee/	*hear ye*	ui	/wee/	*week*
io	/yo/	*Yolanda*	uo	/wo/	*woe*
iu	/yu/	*beauty*	uu	/wu/	*woo*

The diphthongs in the second table are found in Lojban only when used as words by themselves, and in Lojbanized names. Those in the first table may be found anywhere.

Any other time these **vowel pairs** occur together in a single word, they must be kept separate in order to unambiguously distinguish the separate vowels from the diphthongs. The principle has been extended to all Lojban vowels for consistency, and all non-diphthong vowel pairs in a word are separated in print and in sound by an apostrophe ('), representing a short, breathy /h/ sound. (Say *Oh hello* quickly and without a pause between the words to get an English equivalent, in this case of Lojban o'e. Any voiceless non-Lojban sound may also be used.)

When the vowels occur together, one at the end of a word and the other at the beginning of the next word, the ' is not used to separate them. (Were it used, it would join them into a single word). Instead, a pause is mandatory between the two vowels. The pause may be extremely short (called a **glottal stop**) as in the English *he eats*, or may be longer. The pause is mandatory and thus may be inferred without writing it, but it is usually signalled to a reader with a period (.) before the word starting with a vowel.

A pause is also required after any Lojban name, which always ends in a consonant. (A "." is written after the name to mark this, thus distinguishing names from other words without using capitalization.) Every vowel-initial Lojban word is thus preceded by a pause, and such words are usually spelled with a "." at the beginning. There are a small number of other places where pauses are required to separate words. "." may be used to mark the separation in these cases as well.

Lojban words of more than one syllable are stressed on the next-to-last, or **penultimate**, syllable. (The apostrophe counts as a syllable break: blari'o is stressed as blaRI'o.) Syllables for which the vowel is y are not counted in determining penultimate stress, nor are syllables counted in which the letters l, m, n, or r occur in their syllabic forms, with no other vowel in the same syllable. (Thus, lobypli = LO,by,pli, .uacintn. = .UA,cin,tn., kat,rin. = KAT,r,in.) In Lojbanized names, a speaker may retain a semblance of native pronunciation of the name by stressing a non-penultimate syllable. In this case, capitalization is

33

used to mark the abnormal stress, as in DJOsefin. 'Josephine' in the example above.

It is not mandatory to mark stress and pause in writing in Lojban, except for word separation according to the rules above. There is no mandatory intonation, like the rising tone that always accompanies an English question. Lojban equivalents of English intonations are expressed as spoken (and written) words, and may be adequately communicated even in a monotone voice. Such intonation, and pauses for phrasing, are then totally at the speaker's discretion for ease in speaking or being understood, and carry no meaning of their own.

Morphology

The forms of Lojban words are extremely regular. This, coupled with the phonology rules, allows a stream of speech to be uniquely broken down into its component words.

Lojban uses three kinds of words:

cmene	names
brivla	'predicate' words
cmavo	'structure' words

cmene

Names, or *cmene*, are very much like their counterparts in other languages. They are labels applied to things or people, to stand for them in descriptions or in direct address. They may convey meaning in themselves, describing concretely what they are refering to, but do not necessarily do so. Because names are often highly personal and individual, Lojban attempts to allow native language names to be used with a minimum of modification. However, most names must be Lojbanized to some extent, to prevent potential ambiguities. Examples of Lojbanized *cmene* include:

djim.	Jim
djein.	Jane
.arnold.	Arnold

pit.	Pete
katrinas.	Katrina
katr,in.	Catherine
katis.	Cathy
keit.	Kate

cmene may have almost any form, but always end in a consonant, and are followed by a pause. *cmene* are penultimately stressed, unless unusual stress is marked with capitalization. A *cmene* may have multiple parts, each ending with a consonant and pause, or the parts may be combined into a single word with no pause. Thus djan. djonz. /jahn.jonz./ and djandjonz. /JAHNjonz./ are valid (American) Lojbanizations of *John Jones*, while .iunaited. steits. and either .iuNAltet,steits. or .iunaitet,STEITS. are valid Lojbanizations for *United States*, depending on how you wish to stress the name. In the last example, writing the *cmene* as a single word requires capitalization of the stressed syllables /NAI/ or /STEITS/, neither of which is penultimate in the single-word form of the *cmene*.

> **Note:** Lojban words do not allow a **voiced** consonant (like d) to be next to an **unvoiced** consonant (like s), without an intervening pause. This is why the single-word version of *United States* goes into Lojban as .iunaitet,steits., whereas the two-word version remains as is: .iunaited.steits.

The final arbiter of the correct form of the *cmene* is the person doing the naming—although most cultures grant people the right to determine how they want their own name to be spelled and pronounced. The English *Mary* can thus be Lojbanized as meris., maris., meiris., or even marys. The latter is not pronounced much like its English equivalent, but may be desirable to someone who values spelling over pronunciation consistency. The final letter need not be an s; it must, however, be a Lojban consonant of some variety.

cmene are not permitted to have the words la, lai, or doi embedded in them, because they are always preceded by one of these words or by a pause. With one of these words embedded, the *cmene* might break up into valid Lojban words followed by a shorter, incorrect *cmene*. There are similar alternatives to these that can be used in Lojbanization, such as ly, lei, and do'i, that do not cause these problems.

brivla

'Predicate' words, or *brivla*, are the core of Lojban. The concept of 'predicate', or *bridi*, will be discussed in the grammar section below. *brivla* carry most of the semantic information in the language. They serve as the equivalent of English nouns, verbs, adjectives, and adverbs, but are treated identically in Lojban grammar.

brivla may be recognized by several properties:

- they have more than one syllable
- they are penultimately stressed
- they have a consonant cluster (at least two adjacent consonants) within or between the first and second syllables
- they end in a vowel

The consonant cluster rule has the qualification that the letter y is totally ignored, even if it splits a consonant cluster. Thus lobypei /LOBE,uh,pay/ is a *brivla* even though the y separates the bp cluster.

brivla are divided into three subcategories according to how they are created:

gismu	the 'primitive' roots of Lojban; e.g. klama
lujvo	compounds of *gismu*, or their abbreviations, with meanings defined from their components; e.g. lobypli
fu'ivla	'borrowings' from other languages that have been Lojbanized (in a manner similar to how *cmene* are Lojbanized) in order to fit within the *brivla* requirements; e.g. cidjrspageti 'spaghetti' (it's not nearly as hard to say as it looks!)

brivla are defined so as to have only one meaning, which is expressed through a unique *place structure*. This concept is discussed further in the sections on semantics and grammar.

gismu

The *gismu* are the basic roots for the Lojban language. These roots were selected based on various criteria:

- occurrence or word frequency in other languages
- usefulness in building complex concepts
- and a few, like the words gismu, cmavo, and lujvo, are included as uniquely Lojbanic concepts that are basic to the language.

Each *gismu* is exactly five letters long, and has one of two consonant-vowel patterns: CVCCV or CCVCV (e.g. rafsi, bridi). The *gismu* are built so as to minimize listening errors in a noisy environment.

lujvo

When specifying a concept that is not found among the *gismu*, a Lojbanist generally attempts to express the concept as a *tanru*. *tanru* is an elaboration of the concept of 'metaphor' used in English. In Lojban, any *brivla* can be used to modify another *brivla*. The first of the pair modifies the second. Modifier *brivla* may thus be regarded as acting like English adverbs or adjectives. For example, skami pilno is the *tanru* which expresses the concept of 'computer user'.

When a concept expressed in a *tanru* proves useful, or is frequently expressed, it is desirable to choose one of the possible meanings of the *tanru* and assign it to a new, single *brivla*. In the example, we would probably choose the meaning 'user of computers', and form the single *brivla* sampli, out of the *tanru* skami pilno. Such a *brivla*, built from two or more component *gismu*, is called a *lujvo*.

Like *gismu*, however, *lujvo* have only one meaning. Unlike *gismu*, *lujvo* may have more than one form. This is because each *gismu* has between two and five combining forms called *rafsi*, which are joined together in order to form a *lujvo* (e.g. sam and skam for skami; pli and piln for pilno). Longer *rafsi* may be used in place of shorter *rafsi*; the result is considered the same *lujvo*, even though the word is spelled and pronounced differently. Thus brivla, itself a *lujvo* built from the *tanru* bridi valsi, is the same *lujvo* as brivalsi, bridyvla, and bridyvalsi — each using a different combination of *rafsi*.

fu'ivla

The use of *tanru* or *lujvo* is not always appropriate for very concrete or specific terms (e.g. *brie* or *cobra*), or for jargon words specialized to a narrow field (e.g. *quark, integral,* or *iambic pentameter*). These words are in effect 'names' for concepts, and the names were invented by speakers of another language. The vast majority of names for plants, animals, foods, and scientific terminology cannot be easily expressed as *tanru.* They thus must be 'borrowed' (actually 'copied') into Lojban from the original language, forming words called *fu'ivla.*

A borrowed word must be Lojbanized into one of several permitted *fu'ivla* forms. A *rafsi* is then attached to the beginning of the Lojbanized form, usually using a syllabic consonant as 'glue' to ensure that the resulting word is not construed as two separate words. The *rafsi* categorizes or limits the meaning of the *fu'ivla;* otherwise a word having several different jargon meanings in other languages (such as *integral*) would be unclear as to which meaning should be assigned to the *fu'ivla. fu'ivla,* like other *brivla,* are not permitted to have more than one definition.

cmavo

cmavo are the **structure words** that hold the Lojban language together. They often have no concrete meaning in themselves, though they may affect the semantics of *brivla* to which they are attached. *cmavo* include the equivalent of English articles, conjunctions, prepositions, numbers, and punctuation marks.

cmavo are recognized most easily by not being either *cmene* or *brivla.* Thus, they:

- may be a single syllable
- never contain a consonant cluster of any type, whether or not y is counted
- end in a vowel
- need not be penultimately stressed, though they often are if they have more than one syllable

All *cmavo* display one of the following letter patterns, where C stands for a consonant, and V stands for a vowel:

V   VV   V'V   CV   CVV   CV'V

The letter pattern generally does not indicate anything about the grammar of the *cmavo*.

A sequence of *cmavo* can be written without intervening spaces, without any change to its meaning. Such a sequence is called a **compound** *cmavo*. For example, a set of digits comprising a longer number can be written as a single word (e.g. pareci = pa + re + ci = '123').

> **Note:** As far as the stress rules of Lojban are concerned, however, these are still separate words. So you don't have to stress pareci as paREci.

A small number of *cmavo* used in *tanru* have been assigned *rafsi*, so that they may aid in converting those *tanru* into *lujvo*.

Semantics

Lojban is designed to be unambiguous in orthography, phonology, morphology, and grammar. Lojban semantics, however, must support the same breadth of human thought as natural languages. Every human being has different 'meanings' attached to the words they use, based on their unique personal experiences with the concepts involved. So it is impossible to eliminate **semantic ambiguity** (the ambiguity embedded in the variable meanings of words when taken in context) completely.

Rather, Lojban attempts to minimize semantic ambiguity, partly by systematizing as much as possible about semantics, but mostly by removing the clutter and confusion caused by other forms of ambiguity.

brivla

Unlike words in most other languages, a *brivla* has a single meaning, which however may encompass a narrow or broad range of closely related submeanings. *gismu* tend to have more general meanings, while *lujvo* tend to have specific definitions; the compounding of *gismu* into *lujvo* allows expression of any desired degree of specificity. *fu'ivla* have a single narrow meaning.

The semantic definitions of *brivla* are closely tied to the 'predicate' nature of *brivla*, a topic discussed in detail in the grammar section below. In short, a *brivla* defines the relationship between a group of separate but related concepts, called its *sumti*.

brivla are not nouns, verbs, adjectives, or adverbs; yet they incorporate elements of each. These different aspects are brought out in the way the *brivla* is used in the grammar, but the different grammatical environments do not change the meaning of the *brivla*.

brivla are an open-ended set of words; new *lujvo* and *fu'ivla* may be created as needed. Eventually, invented *brivla* will be collected and analyzed, and added to a formal dictionary. The definitions of all *gismu*, including their place structures, have already been specified. The place structure of a *lujvo* can generally be inferred from the place structures of its component *gismu*, using conventions which are generally useful though not hard-and-fast. *fu'ivla* are generally concrete terms, with simple and fairly obvious place structures. When there is uncertainty, listeners can ask about unknown or confusing place structures.

tanru

The heart of Lojban semantics is embedded in *tanru*. The meaning of a *tanru* is somewhat ambiguous: for instance, skami pilno could refer to a computer that is a user, or to a user of computers. There are a variety of ways that the modifier component can be related to the modified component. *cmavo* are used within *tanru* to prevent grammatical ambiguities, such as the various possible groupings of words in a phrase like *pretty little girls school ({pretty {little {girls school}}}, {{pretty little} {girls school}}, {{pretty {little girls}} school}*, and so on).

A speaker may use *tanru* to be arbitrarily general or specific. *tanru* are usually meant to be quite straightforward; *tanru* are always considered as a series of pairs of terms, a **binary metaphor** relationship. In such a relationship the first term by default modifies the second term. The terms may be *brivla*, certain *cmavo* such as numbers, or shorter *tanru*.

Connotation and Assertion

The connotative semantics of Lojban sentences—that is to say, the meaning contained not in the words themselves, but in the associations people make with them—is still relatively undefined. The same is true for the semantics of longer expressions or texts. There is as yet nothing clearly corresponding in Lojban to 'mood' or 'tone', no 'formal' or 'informal' styles, etc.

Because the language is oriented towards logic, the nature of the assertion in a statement, and whether it is true or false, are especially significant. Certain constructs in the language are described as making assertions, and having **truth values** (that is, being true or being false). Other constructs may modify those truth values, and still other constructs are interpreted independently from the truth of the statement.

Grammar

Lojban's grammar is defined by a set of rules that have been tested to be unambiguous using computers. Grammatical unambiguity means that in a grammatical expression, each word has exactly one grammatical interpretation, and that within the expression the words relate grammatically to each other in exactly one way. (By comparison, in the English *Time flies like an arrow*, each of the first three words has at least two grammatical meanings, and each possible combination results in a different grammatical structure for the sentence.)

The **machine grammar** is the set of computer-tested rules that describes, and is the standard for, 'correct Lojban'. If a Lojban speaker follows those rules exactly, the expression will be grammatically unambiguous. If the rules are not followed, ambiguity may exist. Ambiguity does not make communication impossible, of course. Every speaker on Earth speaks an ambiguous language. But Lojbanists strive for accuracy in Lojban grammatical usage, and thereby for grammatically unambiguous communication. (Semantic ambiguity, as we have seen, is another matter.)

It is important to note that new Lojbanists will not be able to speak 'perfectly' when first learning Lojban. In fact, you may never speak perfectly in 'natural' Lojban conversation, even though you achieve fluency in the language. No English speaker always speaks textbook English in natural conversation; Lojban speakers will also make grammatical errors when talking quickly. Lojbanists will, however, be able to speak or write unambiguously *if they are careful*, which is difficult if not impossible with a natural language.

In Lojban grammar rules, words are assembled into short phrases representing a possible piece of a Lojban expression. These phrases are then assembled into longer phrases, and so forth, until all possible pieces have been incorporated through rules that describe all possible expressions in the language. Lojban's rules include grammar for 'incomplete' sentences, for multiple sentences flowing together in a narrative, for quotation, and for mathematical expressions.

The grammar is very simple, but infinitely powerful; often, a more complex phrase can be placed inside a simple structure, which in turn can be used in another instance of the complex phrase structure.

cmavo

The machine grammar includes rules which describe how each word is interpreted. A classification scheme categorizes each word based on what rules it is used in and how it interacts with other words in the grammar. All *cmene* are treated identically by the grammar, as are all *brivla*. The classification divides the *cmavo* of Lojban into about a hundred of these categories of grammar units, called *selma'o*. Whereas the three word types, namely *cmene*, *brivla*, and *cmavo*, are generally considered to correspond to the 'parts of speech' of English, these hundred-odd *selma'o* correspond to the more subtle variations in English grammar, such as the different kinds of pronouns, or the different ways of expressing the past tense of a verb. In this sense, English has hundreds of 'parts of speech'.

Lojban *selma'o* are named after one word within the category, often the one most frequently used. CU, KOhA, PU, and UI are examples of *selma'o*.

> **Note:** The *selma'o* names are capitalized in English discussion of Lojban. The apostrophe is converted to *h* in such usage; this is for compatibility with computer grammar parsers.

bridi

The *bridi* is the basic building block of a Lojban sentence. *bridi* are not words, but concepts. A *bridi* expresses a relationship between several 'arguments', called *sumti*. Those with a background in algebra may recognize the word 'argument' in connection with 'functions', and a *bridi* can be considered a logical 'function' (called a **predicate**) with several 'arguments'. A *brivla* (bridi valsi = *bridi*-word) is a single word which expresses the relationship of a *bridi*.

The definition of a *brivla* includes a specific set of 'places' for *sumti* to be inserted, expressed in a certain order (called a **place structure**) to allow a speaker to clearly indicate which place is which. By convention, we number these places as: x_1, x_2, x_3, x_4, x_5, etc., numbering from the left. Other letters may be used when referring to two or more place structures together.

The unique definition of a *brivla* is thus an enumeration of the component places in order, joined with a description of the relationship between them. The definition of the *gismu* klama 'come, go' can be expressed compactly as:

x_1 comes/goes to x_2 from x_3 via x_4 using x_5

or in full detail:

- x_1 describes a party that acts with result of being in motion;
- x_2 describes a destination where x_1 is located after the action;
- x_3 describes an origin where x_1 is located before the action;
- x_4 describes a route, or points along a route travelled by x_1 between x_2 and x_3;

- x_5 describes the means of transport by which the result is obtained.

Note: The difference between the English verbs *come* and *go* depends on the relationship between x_2 (the destination), x_1 (the origin), and the speaker. The position of the speaker is not part of the Lojban meaning.

When actually using a *brivla* within a *bridi*, it is possible to fill the places (five in the case of klama) with five specific *sumti*. Consider the following example:

Example 1.
le prenu cu klama le zdani le briju le zarci le karce
The person comes/goes to the house from the office via the market using the car.

The definition of the *brivla* used above, klama, shows this relationship. There are five places labelled x_1 through x_5. The *brivla* itself describes how the five places are related, but does not include values for those places. In this example, those places are filled in with five specific *sumti* values:

- x_1 contains le prenu (the person)
- x_2 contains le zdani (the house)
- x_3 contains le briju (the office)
- x_4 contains le zarci (the market)
- x_5 contains le karce (the car)

The *brivla* and its associated *sumti*, used in a sentence, have become a *bridi*. For logicians, the comparable English concept is called a **predication**. In each *bridi*, a *brivla* or *tanru* specifies the relationship between the *sumti*. Such a specification of the relationship, without the *sumti* expressed, is called a *selbri* (**predicate** in English). Whether or not any *sumti* are attached, a *selbri* is found within every *bridi*.

We express a *bridi* relationship in Lojban by filling in the *sumti* places, so that the position of the *sumti* in the place structure is clear, and by expressing the *selbri* that ties the *sumti* together.

It is not necessary to fill in all of the *sumti* to make the sentence meaningful. In English we can say *I go*, without saying where we are going. To say mi klama ("I go...") specifies only one *sumti*; the other four are left unspecified.

In Lojban, we know those four places exist; they are part of the definition of klama. In English, there is no implication that anything is missing, and the sentence *I go* is considered complete. As a *bridi*, mi klama is inherently an incomplete sentence. The omission of defined places in a *bridi* is called **ellipsis**; corresponding ellipsis in the natural languages is a major source of semantic ambiguity. Most Lojban expressions involve some amount of ellipsis. The listener, however, knowing that the omissions have occurred, has a means of asking directly about any specific one of them (or all of them), and resolving the ambiguity. So this kind of semantic ambiguity is not eliminated in Lojban, but it is made more recognizable and more amenable to resolution.

It is permissible to use a *selbri* alone, with no *sumti* filled in, as a very elliptical sentence called an **observative**. The sentence fagri is very similar to the English exclamation *Fire!*, but without the emotional content: it merely states that "something is a fire using some fuel", without explicitly specifying the identity of either.

bridi within *bridi*

You may have noticed that in example (1), each of the *sumti* filling the five places of klama contain a *brivla*. *Each of these brivla are selbri as well*; i.e. they imply a relationship between certain (usually unspecified) *sumti* places. A *selbri* may be labelled with le (among other things) and placed in a *sumti*. When le is used, the concept which the speaker has in mind for the x_1 place of the *selbri* within the *sumti* is understood to fill that *sumti* place. For example, the *sumti* place for le prenu is filled with what the speaker has in mind as being the x_1 place of prenu. Since prenu has the place structure "x_1 is a person", le prenu thus corresponds to 'the person'.

In example (1), there are no places specified for any of the *selbri* embedded in the *sumti*; they are all elliptically omitted, except for the x_1 place, which describes the *sumti* itself. Here is a more complex example:

Example 2.
mi sutra klama le blanu zdani be la djan. le briju
I quickly come to the blue house of John from the office.

More completely, this translates as:

I quickly (at doing something) come to the blue house of John from the office (of someone, at some location), via some route, using some means of travel.

In this example, one of the nested *sumti selbri* has had its places specified, while two places of klama have been elliptically omitted:

- x_1 of sutra klama contains mi (I)
- x_2 of sutra klama contains le blanu zdani be la djan. (the blue-house of the one named John)

  - x_1 of blanu zdani contains the value which fills x_2 of sutra klama; the thing which is a blue house
  - x_2 of blanu zdani contains la djan. (the one named John)

- x_3 of sutra klama contains le briju (the office of someone, at some location)
- The sumti for x_4 and x_5 of sutra klama are elliptically omitted.

Two of the places of the *selbri* in x_3, briju, have also been elliptically omitted, and this is expressed in the more exact translation of the example.

Note that in the two *tanru* in example (2), sutra klama and blanu zdani, each of the four *brivla*may be a self-contained *selbri* unit as well, having its own *sumti* attached to it (using the *cmavo* be). The place structure of the *final* component of a *tanru* (klama and zdani, respectively) becomes the place structure of the *tanru* as a whole, and hence the place structure of the higher level *bridi* structure. (The place structure of klama thus becomes the place structure of the sentence, while the place structure of zdani becomes the place structure of the x_2 *sumti*.)

Place structures

A *brivla* must have a single defined place structure, describing the specific *sumti* places to be related. If this were not so, example (1) might be interpreted arbitrarily; for example, as "The person is the means, the office the route, the market is the time of day, the house is the cause, by which someone elliptically unspecified comes to somewhere (also elliptically unspecified)." Not only is this nonsense, but it is confusing nonsense. With fixed place structures, a Lojbanist will interpret example (1) correctly. A Lojbanist can also, incidentally, express the nonsense just quoted. It will still be nonsense, but it won't be the syntax that confuses the listener; each place will be clearly labelled, and the nonsense can be discussed until resolved.

Thus, for a given *brivla*, or indeed for any *selbri*, we have a specific place structure defined as part of the meaning. Complex *selbri*, described below, simply have more elaborate place structures determined by simple rules from their components.

The place structure of a *bridi* is defined with ordered (and implicitly numbered) places. The *sumti* are typically expressed in this order. When one is skipped, or the *sumti* are presented in a non-standard order, there are various *cmavo* to indicate which *sumti* is which.

Lojban *bridi* are most often given in a sentence as the value of the 1st (x_1) *sumti* place, followed by the *selbri*, followed by the rest of the *sumti* values in order. This resembles the English Subject-Verb-Object (SVO) sentence form. It is shown schematically as:

$[sumti]_{x1} \ [selbri] \ [sumti]_{x2} \ [sumti]_{x3} \ ... \ [sumti]_{xn}$

or abbreviated as:

$x_1 \ selbri \ x_2 \ x_3 \ x_4 \ x_5$

This is the order used for the *bridi* sentences in examples (1) and (2). However, it is equally correct and straightforward to place the *selbri* at the end of the *bridi*:

$x_1 \ x_2 \ x_3 \ x_4 \ x_5 \ selbri$

There are a variety of *cmavo* operators which modify these orders, or which modify one or more pieces of the *bridi*. These can make things quite complicated, yet simple rules allow the listener to take the complications apart, piece by piece, to get the complete and unique structure of the *bridi*. We cannot describe all of these rules here, but a couple of key ones are given.

Of these *cmavo*, cu is placed between a *selbri* and its preceding *sumti* in a sentence-*bridi*. cu cannot be used if there are no *sumti* before the *selbri*; but otherwise it is *always permitted* though *not always required*. Example (1) shows a cu used that is required; example (2) optionally omits the cu. Skill in Lojban includes knowing when cu is required; when it is not required but useful; and when it is permitted, but a distraction.

What happens when the place structure of a given *bridi* does not exactly match the meaning that the speaker is trying to convey? Lojban provides a way to adapt a place structure by adding places to the basic structure. The phrases that do so look exactly like *sumti*, except that they have a *cmavo* marker on the front (called a **modal tag,** or *sumti tcita*) which indicates how the added place relates to the others. The resulting phrase resembles an English prepositional phrase or adverbial phrase, both of which modify a simple English sentence in the same way. Thus I can say:

Example 3. ca le cabdei mi cusku bau la lojban.

- ca le cabdei = an added *sumti*; modal operator ca indicates that the added place specifies 'at the time of...', or 'during...'; thus 'during the nowday', or 'today';
- x_1 = mi (I)
- *selbri* = cusku (x_1 expresses x_2 to x_3 in form/media x_4)
- x_2, x_3, and x_4 are elliptically omitted;
- bau la lojban = an added *sumti*; modal operator bau indicates that the added place specifies 'in language...'; thus 'in language which is called Lojban'.

The sentence thus roughly translates as "Today, I express [it] in Lojban."

Among additional *bridi* places that can be specified are comparison, causality, location, time, the identity of the observer, and the conditions under which the *bridi* is true. In Lojban, semantic components that can apply to any *bridi*, but are not always needed for communication (for instance, location and time), are left optional.

selbri

As described above, the simplest form of *selbri* is a *brivla*. The place structure of the *brivla* is used as the place structure of the *bridi*. Various modifications can be made to the *brivla* and its place structure using *cmavo*. These include ways to treat a single *selbri* as a state, an event, an activity, a property, an amount, etc. For example, jetnu, a *selbri* expressing that x_1 is true, becomes the basis for ka jetnu, a *selbri* expressing the *property* of truth.

Place structures of a *selbri* can undergo 'conversion', which is simply a reordering of the *sumti* places. Since the listener's attention is usually focussed on the first and/or the last *sumti* expressed in the *bridi*, this has a significant effect in relative emphasis, somewhat like the 'passive voice' of English (e.g. *The man was bitten by the dog.* vs. *The dog bit the man.*)

As shown in example (2) above, *tanru* can also be *selbri*. These *tanru* can be composed of simple *brivla, brivla* modified by the techniques referred to above, or simpler *tanru. tanru* themselves can also be modified by the above techniques.

All of the possible modifications to *selbri* are optional semantic components, including tense. (Time and location, and combinations of the two, can be incorporated as tenses in the *selbri*.) With tense unspecified, examples (1) and (2) might be intended as past, present, or future tense; the context determines how the sentence should be interpreted.

sumti

sumti can be compared to the 'subject' and 'object' of English grammar; the value of the first (x_1) *sumti* place resembles the English 'subject'; the other *sumti* are like direct or indirect 'objects'.

But as the discussion of *bridi* above will have indicated, this is only an analogy. *sumti* are not inherently singular or plural: number is one of those semantic components mentioned above that is not always relevant to communication, so number is optional in Lojban. Thus, example (2) could have been translated as *We quickly go/come/went/came (etc.) to the blue houses of those called John.* If this is plausible given the context, but is not the meaning intended, the speaker must add some of the optional semantic information like tense and number, to ensure that the listener can understand the intended meaning. There are several ways to specify number when this is important to the speaker; the numerically unambiguous equivalent of the English plural *people* would be: le su'ore prenu ('the at-least-two persons').

There are a large variety of constructs usable as *sumti*, beyond what we have already seen. Only the most important will be mentioned here. These include:

pro-*sumti*

> *cmavo* which serve as short representations for longer *sumti* expressions (e.g. ko'a 'He/She/It₁', ti 'this'); imperatives are also marked with a pro-*sumti* (ko 'You!');

anaphora/cataphora

> back references and forward references to other sentences and their components (e.g. ri 'the last complete *sumti* mentioned', di'u 'the preceding utterance');

quotations

> grammatical Lojban text, or text in other languages, suitably marked to separate the quote from the rest of the *bridi* (e.g. zo djan 'The word *John*', lu mi klama li'u 'The Lojban text mi klama', zoi by. I go .by. 'The non-Lojban text *I go*');

indirect reference

> reference to something by using its label; among other things, this allows one to talk about another sentence ("That isn't true"), or the state referred to by a sentence ("That didn't happen"), un-ambiguously in all cases (e.g. la'e di'u na fasnu = "The referent of the last sentence does not occur", or "That didn't happen");

named references

> reference to something named by using the name (e.g. la djan 'John', lai ford. '[the mass of things called] Ford');

descriptions

> reference to something by describing it (e.g. le prenu 'the person', le pu crino 'the thing that was green in the past', le nu klama 'the event of going').

Pro-*sumti*, anaphora/cataphora, and indirect references are all equivalent to various uses of pronouns of English, and we won't be going into any further detail here. Quotations and named references are straightforward, and quite similar to their English counterparts. Lojban , however, allows a distinction between Lojban and foreign quotation, and between grammatical and ungrammatical Lojban quotation.

Descriptions appear similar to an English noun phrase (le prenu = 'The person'). For most purposes, this analogy holds. The components of a description are a 'descriptor' or gadri, and a *selbri*. As we've seen, by default such a *sumti* refers to what would be put into the x_1 place (the 'subject') of its *selbri*. Thus le klama is 'the go-er (to some place from some place via some place, using some means of travel)', and le blanu is 'the blue thing'. With conversion, as described above, a speaker can access other places in the *bridi* structure as the new 'subject' or x_1 place: le se klama is "the place gone to (by someone from some place via some place, using some means of travel)". Descriptions are not limited to *selbri* with attached *sumti*; as in example (2), they can include *bridi* with places filled in.

Abstract *bridi* such as events and properties can also be turned into *sumti*. These are among the more common descriptions, and a common source of error among new Lojbanists. If le klama is 'the go-er/come-r (to some place from some place via some place, using some means of travel)', le nu klama is the 'event of (someone) going/coming (to some place from some place via some place, using some means of travel)'. The abstraction treats the *bridi* as a whole rather than isolating the x_1 place.

Descriptions can also incorporate sentences based on abstracts; this is needed to elaborate *sumti* like le nu klama. For example, le nu mi klama ti is 'the event that: I come here (from some place via some place, using some means of travel)', or simply 'my coming here'.

In addition to number, Lojban allows for mass concepts to be treated as a unit. This is equivalent to English mass concepts as used in sentences like *Water is wet*, and *People are funny*. Mass description also allows a speaker to distinguish, in sentences like *Two men carried the log across the field*, whether they did it together, or whether they did it separately (as in "One carried it across, and the other carried it back.")

Sets can be described in *sumti*, as well as logically and non-logically connected lists of *sumti*. Thus, Lojban provides for: "Choose the coffee, the tea, or the milk", or "Choose exactly one from the set of {coffee, tea, milk}". Note that English connectives are not truly logical. The latter is the common interpretation of "Coffee, tea, or milk?" and is relatively unambiguous. The former, if translated literally into Lojban, would be a different statement, because of the ambiguous meaning of English *or*.

Finally, *sumti* can be qualified using time, location, modal operators, or various other means of identification. Incidental notes can be thrown in, and pro-*sumti* can have values assigned to them. Lojban also has constructions that are similar to the English possessive.

Free Modifiers

Free modifiers are grammatical constructs that can be inserted in a *bridi*, without changing the meaning, or the truth value, of the *bridi*. Free modifiers include the following types of structures:

parentheses
Parenthetical notes, which can be of any length, as long as they are grammatical.

vocatives
These are used for direct address; they include several expressions used for 'protocol', allowing for smooth, organized communications in disruptive environments (e.g. ta'a 'excuse me', be'e 'are you listening?'), as well as some expressions that are associated with courtesy in most languages.

discursives
These are comments made at a metalinguistic level about the sentence, and about its relationship to other sentences. In English, certain adverbs and conjunctions serve this function (e.g. *however, but, in other words*).

discursive *bridi*
These are halfway between discursives and parentheses, and allow the speaker to make metalinguistic statements about a sentence without modifying that sentence. Thus, the discursive

bridi equivalent of *This sentence is false* does not result in a paradox, since it would be expressed as a discursive *bridi* inside of another sentence, the one actually being described.

attitudinals

These are expressions of emotion and attitude about the sentence, being expressed discursively. They are similar to the English exclamations like *Oh!* and *Ahhhh!*, but they include a much broader range of possibilities, covering a range comparable to that expressed by English intonation; they can also serve as indicators of intensity. Also included in this category are indicators of the relationship between the speaker and the expression (**evidentials**). Found in native American languages among others, these allow the hearer to judge how seriously to take an assertion, by making explicit the basis for the speaker making the assertion: that the speaker directly observed what is being reported, heard about it from another, deduced it, etc.

Questions

The manner of asking questions in Lojban is quite different from English. In Lojban, most questions are asked by placing a question word in place of the value to be filled in by the person answering. The question word mo can be used in the grammatical place of any *bridi*, including those within *sumti*. It asks for a *bridi* (usually a *selbri*) to be supplied which correctly fills in the space. It is thus similar to English *what?* This booklet is titled la lojban. mo, meaning 'The thing called Lojban is what?', or, of course, 'What is Lojban?' The question word ma is used in place of a *sumti* in the same manner. Thus a listener can ask for ellipsis to be filled in, or can pose new questions that are similar to the classic English questions (*who?, when?, where?, how?,* and *why?*).

Yes/no questions can either be asked as a question of emotional attitude—such as belief, certitude, supposition, decision, approval, or intention—or as a question of truth and falsity. In the first case, the answer is an attitudinal. In the second case, the answer is an assertion or denial of the *bridi* being queried. Lojban also provides question words that can request a value filling many other grammatical functions.

Tenses

The tense system of Lojban expresses not only the time at which something happens, but also the place. It can express very complex combinations of both temporal and spatial distances and directions (the time directions being 'past' and 'future', of course), interval sizes and ranges, and parts of events such as 'beginning', 'middle', and 'end'. Fortunately, this entire system is optional: it is perfectly correct to express *bridi* with no specific tense at all, in which case the place and time is up to the listener to figure out.

Some examples of tenses in use are:

- mi ca ba'o cadzu "I have now walked"
- mi ri'u va cadzu "I walk around somewhere on the right, at some medium distance"
- and the formidable mi pu zu ze'i mo'i te'e cadzu "A long time ago in the past, I walked for a short time along the edge."

Logic and Lojban

Lojban supports all of the standard truth-functions of predicate logic. These can be used to connect any of several different levels of construct: *sumti, bridi, selbri*, sentences, etc.; the methods used indicate unambiguously what is being joined. As an example of English ambiguity in the scope of logical connectives, the incomplete sentence *I went to the window and ...* can be completed in a variety of different ways (e.g. *...closed it, ...the door, ...Mary went to the desk*); in these, the *and* is joining a variety of different constructs. You must hear and analyze the whole sentence to interpret the *and*, and you still may not be certain of having a correct understanding. Lojban would make clear the structures being joined from the outset.

Another way Lojban supports logical connectives is by distinguishing them from non-logical connectives. The latter include:

- the *and* of mixing (as in "coffee with milk" — which is neither just coffee nor just milk, but both at once);
- expressions of causality (Lojban supports expression of four different kinds of causality: physical causation, motivation, justification, and logical implication);
- and the various conjunctive discursives (such as *but*, and *however*), which in English imply 'and' without stating it.

Mathematics

Lojban has incorporated a detailed grammar for mathematical expressions. This grammar parallels the predicate grammar of the non-mathematical language. Numbers may be clearly expressed, including exponential and scientific notation. Digits are provided for decimal and hexadecimal arithmetic, and letters may be used for additional digits if desired. There is a distinction made between mathematical operations and mathematical relations. The set of operations is not limited to 'standard arithmetic'. Operations therefore assume a left-grouping precedence which can be overridden with parentheses, or optionally included precedence labels that override this grouping on evaluating the expression.

Included in Lojban are means to express non-mathematical concepts and quantities as numbers, and mathematical relationships as ordinary *bridi*. In Lojban, it is easy to talk about a 'brace' of oxen or a 'herd' of cattle, as well as to discuss the "5 fingers of your hand", or "∫ $-2x^3+x^2-3x+5$ dx evaluated over the interval of −5 to +5 bottles of water".

> **Note:** In case you're curious: li ri'o ni'u re pi'i xy. bi'e te'a ci su'i xy. bi'e te'a re vu'u ci bi'e pi'i xy. su'i muboi ge'a xy.boi ge'a mo'e vei ni'u mu bi'o ma'u mu ve'o djacu botpi

selsku

The set of possible Lojbanic expressions is called selsku. Lojban has a grammar for multiple sentences tied together as narrative text, or as a conversation; the unambiguous Lojban grammar supports an indefinite string of Lojban paragraphs of arbitrary length. Using the rules of this grammar, multiple speakers can use, define, and redefine pro-*sumti*. Paragraphs, chapters, and even books can be separately distinguished: each can be numbered or titled distinctly. One can express logical and non-logical connectives over multi-sentence scope. (This is the essence of a set of instructions—a sequence of closely-related sentences.) Complex sets of suppositions can be expressed, as well as long chains of reasoning based on logical deduction. In short, the possibilities of Lojban grammatical expression are endless.

Chapter 3. Diagrammed Summary of Lojban Grammar

xracartu torvelski be le lojbo gerna

This chapter gives diagrammed examples of basic Lojban sentence structures. The most general pattern is covered first, followed by successive variations on the basic components of the Lojban sentence. There are many more capabilities not covered in these examples. A Lojban glossary will be found at the end of this section.

The Lojban sentence structure

A Lojban sentence expresses a relationship (*bridi*), normally claiming that the relationship holds (that it is 'true'). A *bridi* relationship consists of several ideas or objects called **arguments** (*sumti*), which are related by a **predicate relation** (*selbri*). The following uses the Lojban terms *bridi*, *sumti*, and *selbri*, because it is best to come to understand them independent of the English associations of the corresponding words.

Some words used as *sumti*

mi   I/me/my, we/us/our
do   you/your
ti   this/this-here/this one, these/these here/these ones
ta   that/that-there/that one, those/those ones
tu   that yonder, those yonder
zo'e unspecified value (used when a *sumti* is unimportant or obvious)

sumti are not specific as to number (singular or plural), nor gender (masculine/feminine/neuter). Such distinctions can be optionally added.

Names may be expressed as *sumti*, labelled with la:

la meris. the one/ones named Mary

la djan. the one/ones named John

(Other Lojban spelling variations are possible for names imported from other languages.)

Some words used to indicate *selbri* relations

vecnu x_1 (seller) sells x_2 (goods) to x_3 (buyer) for x_4 (price)

tavla x_1 (talker) talks to x_2 (audience) about x_3 (topic) in language x_4

blari'o x_1 (object/light source) is blue-green

melbi x_1 (object/idea) is beautiful to x_2 (observer) by standard x_3

We will describe these and other possible *sumti* and *selbri* in more detail below.

Conventions

The following conventions will be used to show the structure of Lojban sentences in diagrams:

- The *selbri* relation will *be italicized.*
- The *sumti* arguments will <u>be underlined</u>.
- Optional separator/terminator words are placed in square brackets. They may be omitted if so bracketed. The general rule is that these may be omitted if and only if no grammatical ambiguity results. Each such word serves as an end marker for particular structures, making the overall structure of the sentence clear.
- The structure of Lojban phrases is indicated by bars beneath the text, joining related words together.
- Words modifying other words are indicated by arrows pointing from the modifier to the modified.

Basic structure of a Lojban sentence

<u>sumti</u> <u>sumti</u> ... <u>sumti</u> [cu] *selbri* <u>sumti</u> <u>sumti</u> ... <u>sumti</u> [vau]

- Normally, there must be at least one *sumti* before the *selbri*.

- Each *selbri* relation has a specifically defined **place structure** that defines the role of each *sumti* in the *bridi* relationship, based on its position in order. In the examples above, that order was expressed by labelling the positions x_1, x_2, x_3, and x_4.

- cu acts as a separator after at least one preceding *sumti* to clearly mark the *selbri*. As the diagram indicates, it may often be omitted. There will be examples of this below.

- vau goes at the end of the sentence, indicating that no more *sumti* will follow. It usually may be omitted.

Sentence examples

mi	[cu]	*vecnu*	ti	ta
seller-x_1		sells	goods-sold-x_2	buyer-x_3
I		sell	this	to that

zo'e	[vau]
price-x_4	
for some price.	(No more *sumti*)

I sell this-thing/these-things to that-buyer/those-buyers. (The price is obvious or unimportant.)

- Both the cu and the vau are optional in this example and could be omitted

- When an unspecified *sumti* (zo'e) is at the end of a sentence, it may be omitted.

- Normally, there will be one *sumti* (the x_1) before the *selbri*. There may be more than one:

mi	ti	[cu]	*vecnu*	ta
seller-x_1	goods-sold-x_2		sells	buyer-x_3
I	this		sell	to that.

[vau]

(No more *sumti*)

Translates as stilted or poetic English: *I, this thing, do sell to that buyer.*

Usually, more than one *sumti* will be placed before the *selbri* for style or for emphasis on the *sumti* displaced from their normal position. (Native speakers of languages other than English may prefer such orders.)

Observatives

If there is no *sumti* before the *selbri*, then it is understood that the x_1 *sumti* value is equivalent to zo'e; i.e. it is unimportant or obvious, and therefore omitted. Any *sumti* after the *selbri* start counting from x_2, x_3, x_4...:

<u>ta</u>	[cu]	*melbi*	[vau]
object/idea-x_1		is-beautiful	(to someone by some standard)
That/Those		is/are beautiful.	

That is beautiful. (or) *Those are beautiful.*

When the x_1 is omitted:

—	*melbi*	[vau]
(Unspecified)	is-beautiful	(to someone by some standard)

Beautiful! (or) *It's beautiful!*

—	*vecnu*	<u>ti</u>	<u>ta</u>	[vau]
(Unspecified)	sells	this	to that.	

(Look!) Someone's selling this to that!

Omitting the x_1 adds emphasis to the *selbri* relation, which has become first and foremost in the sentence. This kind of sentence is termed an **observative**, because it is usually stated by someone when they first *observe* or take note of the relation, and wish to quickly

communicate it to someone else. Commonly understood English ob-
servatives include *Smoke!* upon seeing smoke or smelling the odor, or
Car! to a person crossing the street who might be in danger. Any
Lojban *selbri* can be an observative if no *sumti* appear before the *selbri*.

cu does not occur in an observative; cu is a **separator**, and there must
be a *sumti* before the *selbri* that needs to be kept separate, for it to be
used. With no *sumti* preceding the *selbri*, cu is not permitted.

True/false (yes/no) questions (the word xu)

xu question sentence (Is-it-true-that...):

xu	**mi**	**[cu]**	*vecnu*	**ti**	**ta**	**[vau]**
Is-it-true?	I		sell	this	that.	

Is it true that I sell this to that?

xu has a very unrestricted grammar, and is permitted virtually
anywhere in a sentence. At the beginning of the sentence, xu asks
about the truth of the *bridi* relationship. Elsewhere, in a sentence, xu
attaches to the immediately preceding word (or the structure implied
by that preceding word, when it is the marker for a structure). Thus,
also after the vau ending the sentence, xu would ask about the entire
bridi (the vau cannot be omitted if xu is to appear 'after' it).

xu appearing after a *sumti* questions whether the *bridi* relationship
expressed by the sentence is true for that *sumti* value in particular:

mi	**[cu]**	*vecnu*	**ti**	**xu**	**ta**	**[vau]**
				←		
I		sell	this	Is-it-true?	that.	

Is it true that I sell this (as opposed to something else) to that?

Similarly, xu following vecnu in the above example would question the
truth of the *bridi* relationship by specifically asking whether 'sell' is a
true relation between the *sumti*.

We will discuss how to answer a xu true/false question below in the
section on *selbri*.

Varying *sumti* order

There are ways to vary the order of *sumti* from the numerical order specified by the place structure. A *sumti* may be placed out of numerical order by labelling it in front with a tag indicating the actual numerical position of the *sumti* in the place structure. The structure is thus of the form FA *sumti* (where the FA category word shows which of the existing *sumti* places is being used, by number):

fa '1st *sumti*: x_1'

fe '2nd *sumti*: x_2'

fi '3rd *sumti*: x_3'

fo '4th *sumti*: x_4'

fu '5th *sumti*: x_5'

One reason for using these tags is to skip a place structure place without having to insert a zo'e for each skipped place:

<u>mi</u>	[cu]	*tavla*	fo	<u>la lojban.</u>
talker		talk	x_4=language	
I		talk	in language	Lojban.

[vau]
I talk in Lojban (to someone about some topic).

which is equivalent to:

<u>mi</u>	[cu]	*tavla*	<u>zo'e</u>	<u>zo'e</u>
talker		talk	audience	topic
I		talk	to unspecified	about unspecified

<u>la lojban.</u>				[vau]
language				
in Lojban.				

I talk in Lojban (to someone about some topic).

After a FA tag sets the place number, any later *sumti* places continue the numbering consecutively:

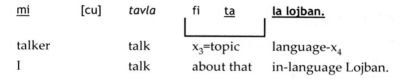

m̲i̲	[cu]	*tavla*	fi	t̲a̲	l̲a̲ l̲o̲j̲b̲a̲n̲.
talker		talk	x_3=topic		language-x_4
I		talk	about that		in-language Lojban.

[vau]
I talk about that in Lojban (to someone unspecified).

Another reason to use FA tags is to change emphasis; listeners focus most closely on the *sumti* at the beginning of a sentence.

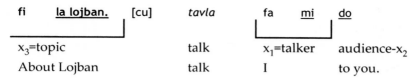

fi	l̲a̲ l̲o̲j̲b̲a̲n̲.	[cu]	*tavla*	fa	m̲i̲	d̲o̲
x_3=topic			talk	x_1=talker		audience-x_2
About Lojban			talk	I		to you.

[vau]
It's Lojban that I talk to you about (in an unspecified language).

There are other ways of rearranging the *sumti* of a sentence that will be discussed below.

Note that in all examples where a *sumti* is omitted, there is an unspoken and unspecified value for each of the omitted place structure places.

An observative can be formed by using fa to move the first (x_1) *sumti* to the position after the *selbri*.

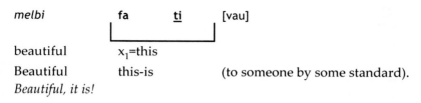

melbi	fa	t̲i̲	[vau]
beautiful	x_1=this		
Beautiful	this-is		(to someone by some standard).

Beautiful, it is!

Basic structure of an utterance

People usually don't say just one sentence. Lojban has a specific structure for talk or writing that is longer than one sentence. The entirety of a given speech event or written text is called an **utterance**.

sentence .i sentence .i sentence [...] .i sentence
ni'o sentence .i sentence .i sentence .i sentence [...] .i sentence
ni'o sentence .i sentence [...] .i sentence
[fa'o]

- ni'o separates **paragraphs** (covering different topics of discussion). In a long text or utterance, the topical structure of the text may be indicated by multiple ni'os, with perhaps ni'oni'oni'o used to indicate a chapter, ni'oni'o to indicate a section, and a single ni'o to indicate a subtopic corresponding to a single English paragraph.
- .i separates sentences. .i is sometimes compounded with words that modify the exact meaning (the semantics) of the sentence within the utterance. xu, discussed above, is one such word — it turns the sentence from a statement to a question of truth. When more than one person is talking, a new speaker will usually omit the .i even though she/he may be continuing on the same topic. It is still OK for a new speaker to say the .i before continuing; indeed it is encouraged for maximum clarity (since it is possible the second speaker might merely be adding words onto the end of the first speaker's sentence). A good translation for .i is the *and* used in run-on sentences when people are talking informally: "I did this, and then I did that, and ..., and ...".
- fa'o is an optional end-of-utterance marker, used primarily in computer input. It is not needed in human speech.

You may now see why the vau at the end of the sentence can generally be omitted. Since the following word will usually be an .i or a ni'o starting a new sentence or paragraph, there is no possibility of ambiguity if it is omitted. These separators prevent the *sumti* at the beginning of the next sentence from being mistaken as a trailing *sumti* of this sentence.

Punctuation

Lojban has no mandatory punctuation marks. Because Lojban speech *exactly* matches the written text representing that speech, all 'punctuation' that is used in English to show sentence structure, questions, exclamations or tone of voice, and even quotations must be expressed in Lojban as actual words.

The special use of the apostrophe, period, capitalization and commas is outlined in *Overview of Lojban Grammar*.

> **Tip:** Some optional conventions allow certain punctuation symbols to appear to clarify printed text, making it easier to read. (Such punctuation is not considered part of the standard Lojban orthography, and is not accepted by all Lojbanists.) These punctuation symbols *always* appear in conjunction with the printed word representing that punctuation symbol, rather than replacing it. Thus a xu question may be marked with a question mark immediately after the xu (or immediately before the xu, possibly inverted, as in Spanish). Other questions may similarly be marked with a question mark after the word indicating the question—*not* at the end of the sentence. There are words that may be associated with exclamation points, start of quotation (represented by «) and end of quotation (»). For example:
>
> .i xu? do klama
> .i ?xu do bacru «lu mi klama li'u» bau la lojban.
> .i ¿xu .ue! do bacru «lu do bacru «lu mi klama li'u» bau la lojban. li'u»

The Basic Components (*sumti* and *selbri*)

We now discuss the substructures of the basic components that make up a sentence. Any variety of *selbri* may be placed in a sentence, or in another substructure below it that contains *selbri*. Likewise, any variety of *sumti* may be placed in a sentence, or in another substructure below it that contains *sumti*. You may see that this can potentially lead to extremely complicated structures nested within one another. Lojban's unambiguous grammar allows even these most complicated structures to be untangled in only one way.

Simple *sumti*

sumti are not specific as to number (singular or plural), nor gender (masculine/feminine/neuter). Such distinctions can be optionally expressed by being more specific.

'pronoun' *sumti*

These expressions (usually called pro-*sumti* in Lojban) include the single-word *sumti* given above:

mi	I/we
do	you
ti	this/these
ta	that/those
tu	that/those-yonder
zo'e	something unspecified (it's either obvious or unimportant)

Some other words in this category include:

ri	he/she/it (the-last-referenced-*sumti*)
ko	**imperative** you
ko'a	it/he/she/they (a specific value)
di'u	it/this (the last sentence)

There are many others, each with a particular meaning. For example, there are 9 other words related to ko'a. Each may be used to represent a separate value of *it*. Since Lojban has no gender or number, these 10 words represent *he*, *she*, and *they* as well, and it becomes more clear why so many are needed to keep track of distinct entities.

zo'e is a place-filler *sumti*, allowing you to skip over a *sumti* place in the ordered place structure without specifying a value. The speaker indicates that there is a value, but that it is not important to specify it, or that the speaker thinks it is obvious given the context.

<u>do</u>	[cu]	*tavla*	**zo'e**	<u>ti</u>	[vau]
You		talk		about this.	

You talk about this (to someone, in some language.)

ri is a quick back-reference *sumti*. It can have a new meaning, depending on the context, every time it occurs. The rules for counting back to 'the last *sumti*' include some special cases that can't be covered in this summary, but in most simple sentences, the referent will be obvious. There are two other back-referencing *sumti* of this type.

mi	[cu]	*tavla*	fi	la lojban.	ri
I		talk		x_3=about-Lojban	in-it(=Lojban)-x_4.

[vau]
I talk about Lojban in Lojban (to someone unspecified.)

ko is used to express commands. A statement with ko can be interpreted by replacing the ko with do, and then taking the result as a command to the listener to make the sentence true, with himself/herself considered as do:

ko	[cu]	*tavla*	mi	[vau]
You (imperative)		talk	to-me.	

Talk to me!

is the command equivalent of:

do	[cu]	*tavla*	mi	[vau]
You		talk	to-me.	

You talk to me.

ko need not be in the first position in the *bridi*, but rather can occur anywhere a *sumti* is allowed, leading to possible Lojban commands that are very unlike English commands:

mi	[cu]	*tavla*	ko	[vau]
I		talk	to-you (imperative)	

Let me talk (to you)!

ko is even permitted to occur in more than one place in a sentence, allowing for meaning-rich commands like:

<u>**ko**</u>	[cu]	*tavla*	<u>**ko**</u>	[vau]
You (imp.)		talk	to-you (imp.)	

Talk to yourself!

The English misses some of the meaning, since the Lojban expresses two commands at once: that the listener talk to herself, but also that the listener allow herself to be talked-to (by herself).

Names ("la name")

Lojban names always end with a consonant followed by a mandatory pause (which may be very short). No other Lojban word ends with a consonant. Thus names are easily recognized by both their form, and by being marked with a preceding la.

<u>do</u>	[cu]	*tavla*	<u>**la mark.**</u>	<u>ti</u>	[vau]
You		talk	to-Mark	about this.	

You talk to Mark about this.

Question *sumti* ("ma")

ma indicates a question about the value of a *sumti*. It is answered by 'filling in the blank', replacing the ma with the intended *sumti* value. It can be translated as *Who?* or *What?* in most cases, but also serves for *When?*, *Where?*, and *Why?* when used in *sumti* places that express time, location, or cause.

<u>**ma**</u>	[cu]	*tavla*	<u>do</u>	[vau]
__?		talks	to-you.	

What/Who talks to you?

is answerable by:

<u>mi</u>	[cu]	*tavla*	<u>do</u>	[vau]
I talk to you.				

Like ko, ma can occur in any position where a *sumti* is allowed, not just in the first position:

<u>do</u>   [cu]   *tavla*   **ma**   [vau]
You talk to what/whom? (What/who do you talk to?)

ma can also appear in multiple *sumti* positions in one sentence, in effect asking several questions at once.

ma   [cu]   *tavla*   **ma**   [vau]
What/Who talks to what/whom?

The two separate ma positions ask two separate questions, and can therefore be answered with different values in each *sumti* place.

Description *sumti* ("le *selbri* [ku]")

le specifies a *sumti* that the speaker has in mind more completely than the pro-*sumti* we have seen. It does so by introducing a *bridi* relationship that the *sumti* in question forms the first (x_1) *sumti* of. This *bridi* is represented by its corresponding *selbri*. Description *sumti* phrases have a terminator at their conclusion, ku, which is omitted when no ambiguity results.

<u>mi</u>   [cu]   *tavla*   **le vecnu [ku]**
I   talk   to the seller

le blari'o [ku]   [vau]
about the blue-green thing.

le vecnu takes the *selbri* vecnu, which has the 'seller' in the x_1 place, and uses it in this sentence to describe a particular 'seller' that the speaker has in mind (one that she probably expects the listener will also know about). Similarly, the speaker has a particular blue-green thing in mind, which is described using le to mark blari'o, a *selbri* whose first *sumti* is something blue-green.

There are many variations on le *sumti* [ku] constructs, but to discuss them, we must first discuss the more complex structures of *selbri*.

selbri structure

Though Lojban sentences often translate word-for-word into fairly clear English, *selbri* relations are actually quite unlike English. For example, the *selbri* bajra expresses a relation of running.

sumti	*bajra*	*sumti*	*sumti*	*sumti*
runner	[running]	on-surface	using-limbs	with-gait

In some sentence positions, bajra might be interpreted as the 'verb' *to run*; in other positions, as the 'noun' or 'adjective' *running*. In le *sumti* [ku], described in the preceding section, it represents the 'noun' interpretation of its x_1 *sumti* place: 'runner'. (Some English words, like *cook*, have similar properties, but the analogy is weak.)

brivla

The simplest form of *selbri* is an individual word. A word which may by itself express a *selbri* relation is called a *brivla*. The three types of *brivla* are *gismu* (root words), *lujvo* (compounds), and *fu'ivla* (borrowings from other languages). All have identical grammar; they are allowed wherever any *selbri* appear in these examples.

gismu

mi	[cu]	*klama*	ti	zo'e	zo'e
Go-er		goes	destination	origin	route

ta				[vau]	

means.

I go here (to this) using that means (from somewhere via some route).

lujvo

ta	[cu]	*blari'o*	[vau]
That		is-blue-green.	

fu'ivla

ta	[cu]	*cidjrspageti*	[vau]
That		is-spaghetti.	

Some short words may serve as *selbri*, acting as variables that stand for another *selbri*. The most commonly used of these is go'i, which represents the main *bridi* of the previous Lojban sentence, with any new *sumti* or other features in the sentence replacing those in the previous sentence. Thus:

ta	[cu]	*go'i*	[vau]
That		too/same-as-last *selbri*.	

That (is spaghetti), too.

When the word go'i by itself refers back to a *bridi* marked as a xu true/false question, it repeats that *bridi*, thereby claiming it is true. Thus, in this sense only, go'i can mean 'yes'. xu questions can also be answered 'yes' by repeating the entire sentence in full, but go'i is much easier to say:

xu	ta	[cu]	blari'o	[vau]
Is-it-true-that that is-blue-green?				

go'i	[vau]
True. (repeats "That is blue-green.")	

Contradictory negation ("na *selbri*")

The negation particle na can occur at the beginning of any *selbri*. It says that the relation claimed by the *selbri* does not hold (this is called **contradictory negation**). It may often be translated as "It is false that [sentence]".

mi	[cu]	na	klama	ti	ta	[vau]
		FALSE				

It is false that I go to this from that.

The na is only permitted at the beginning of a *complete selbri*. It is considered part of the *selbri* in other constructs in the language, but is disallowed from other positions within a *tanru* (discussed below).

If the contradictory negation particle na precedes go'i, the combination na go'i denies the relation claimed by go'i. Thus, after a xu true/false question, na go'i expresses the answer "False", or "No".

If you were to use go'i after a sentence that contained a na contradictory negation, the negation would carry over to the repeated sentence. Unlike English, na go'i would *not* form a double negative; it merely replaces the na by another na leaving the sentence unchanged. Instead, you must cancel a negative by using the positive equivalent of na, ja'a, to replace the na in the previous sentence:

<u>mi</u>   [cu]   **ja'a**   *go'i*   [vau]
                        TRUE

It is true that I do (go to this from that).

Scalar negation ("na'e-word *brivla*")

na deals primarily with the truth or falsity of a *bridi*. Lojban also supports a separate form of negation, called **contrary** or **scalar negation**. A scalar negation attaches tightly to the next *brivla* of the *selbri*, modifying the meaning of the word on some scale. Scalar negation structures may appear anywhere where a *brivla* or *selbri* is allowed. Scalar negation words include na'e (other than), to'e (absolute opposite of), and no'e (neutral on the scale); je'a is a strong positive scale assertion, translating roughly as 'certainly' or 'indeed':

Positive		Neutral	Negative	
je'a	—	no'e	na'e	to'e

Examples:

<u>mi</u>   [cu]   *melbi*   [vau]
I am beautiful.

<u>mi</u>   [cu]   *na'e melbi*   [vau]
I am other-than beautiful.

<u>mi</u>	[cu]	*to'e melbi*	[vau]

I am ugly/opposite-of-beautiful.

<u>mi</u>	[cu]	*no'e melbi*	[vau]

I am plain/neutral on the beauty–ugliness scale.

<u>mi</u>	[cu]	*je'a melbi*	[vau]

I am indeed beautiful.

Question *selbri* ("mo")

mo, like its *sumti* relative ma, is a fill-in-the-blank question. It asks the respondent to provide a *selbri* that would give a true relation if inserted in place of the mo:

<u>do</u>	[cu]	*mo*	[vau]

You are-what/do-what?

mo may be used *anywhere* a *brivla* or other *selbri* might be. Keep this in mind for later examples. Unfortunately, by itself, mo is a very nonspecific question. The response to the above question could be:

<u>mi</u>	[cu]	*melbi*	[vau]

I am beautiful.

or:

<u>mi</u>	[cu]	*tavla*	[vau]

I talk.

Clearly, mo requires some cooperation between the speaker and the respondent to ensure that the right question is being answered. If context doesn't make the question specific enough, the speaker must ask the question more specifically using a more complex construction such as *tanru* (below).

It is perfectly permissible for the respondent to fill in other unspecified places in responding to a mo question. Thus, the respondent in the last example could have also specified an audience, a topic, and/or a language in the response:

mi	[cu]	*tavla*	do	la lojban.	[vau]

I am talking to you about Lojban.

Conversion ("se-word *brivla*")

se and others in its word-category modify a *brivla* used in a *selbri* by changing the order of the *sumti* that are attached. This results in a new *selbri* that expresses the same relation, but with different order of emphasis. se exchanges the first and second *sumti* places of the un-modified *brivla*. This reversal is called **conversion**.

The *bridi* sentence:

do	[cu]	*vecnu*	ta	mi
seller-x_1		sells	thing-sold-x_2	buyer-x_3

zo'e	[vau]
price-x_4.	

You sell that to me.

can be converted to:

ta	[cu]	*se vecnu*	do	mi
thing sold-x_1		is-sold-by	seller-x_2	buyer-x_3

zo'e	[vau]
price-x_4.	

That is sold by you to me.

The effect is similar to what in English is called 'passive voice'. In Lojban, however, a conversion is *not* 'passive': the converted *selbri* has a place structure that is renumbered to reflect the place reversal, thus having effects when such a conversion is used in combination with other constructs (such as fi and le *selbri* [ku]).

The other simple relatives of se are: te (switches 1st and 3rd places), ve (switches 1st and 4th places), and xe (switches 1st and 5th places). The effects of using them may be seen on the 5-place *gismu selbri*, klama:

go-er	goes	to desti-nation	from origin	via route	using means
x_1	*klama*	x_2	x_3	x_4	x_5
destination	is-gone-to	**by go-er**	from origin	via route	using means
x_1	*se klama*	x_2	x_3	x_4	x_5
origin	is-gone-from	to desti-nation	**by go-er**	via route	using means
x_1	*te klama*	x_2	x_3	x_4	x_5
route	is-gone-via	to desti-nation	from origin	**by go-er**	using means
x_1	*ve klama*	x_2	x_3	x_4	x_5
means	is-used-to-go	to desti-nation	from origin	via route	**by go-er**
x_1	*xe klama*	x_2	x_3	x_4	x_5

tanru ("modifier-*selbri* modified-*selbri*")

tanru are compound *selbri*—constructions of multiple *brivla/selbri* components. Each component might be a single word, or it might be a word modified by place structure converters (like se), or scalar negations (like na'e). *tanru* take *selbri* components (including other *tanru*) in pairs, with the first part modifying the second part.

The kind of modification is vague: *tanru* may act like an English adjective–noun (*fast-runner*), adverb–verb (*quickly-run*) or it may restrict a larger set (*runner-shoes*). Context will generally indicate what is a plausible interpretation of a *tanru*. You should allow for creative interpretation: 'runner-shoes' might be interpreted in some imaginative instances as 'shoes that run by themselves'. In general, however, the meaning of a *tanru* is determined by the *literal* meaning of its components, and not by any connotations or figurative meanings. So sutra tavla 'fast-talker' would not necessarily imply any trickery or deception, and a jikca toldi 'social butterfly' must always be an insect with large brightly-colored wings, of the family *lepidoptera*.

The place structure of a *tanru* is always that of the final *brivla* or final component of the *tanru*. Thus, the following has the place structure of klama:

<u>mi</u>	[cu]	*sutra klama*	<u>la meris.</u>	[vau]

I quickly-go to Mary.

With the conversion se klama in the final position, the place structure is that of se klama: the x_1 place is the destination, and the x_2 place is the go-er:

<u>mi</u>	[cu]	*sutra se klama*	<u>la meris.</u>	[vau]

I quickly am-gone-to by Mary.

A similar example shows that there is more to conversion than merely switching places, though:

<u>la tam.</u>	[cu]	*melbi tavla*	<u>la meris.</u>	[vau]

Tom beautifully-talks to Mary (or) *Tom is a beautiful-talker to Mary.*

has the place structure of tavla, but note the two distinct interpretations.

Now, using conversion, we can modify the place structure order:

<u>la meris.</u>	[cu]	*melbi se tavla*	<u>la tam.</u>	[vau]

Mary is beautifully-talked-to by Tom (or) *Mary is a beautiful-audience for Tom.*

and we see that the modification has been changed so as to focus on Mary's role in the *bridi* relationship, leading to a different set of possible interpretations.

Note that there is no place structure change if the modifying term is converted, and hence there is less drastic variation in possible meanings:

| <u>la tam.</u> | [cu] | ***tavla melbi*** | <u>la meris.</u> | [vau] |

Tom is talker-wise–beautiful according to Mary.

| <u>la tam.</u> | [cu] | ***se tavla melbi*** | <u>la meris.</u> | [vau] |

Tom is audience-wise–beautiful according to Mary.

The manner in which Tom is seen as beautiful by Mary changes, but Tom is still the one perceived as beautiful, and Mary, the observer of beauty.

Any *selbri* form can be used in either position of a *tanru*. This allows more specific mo questions to be formulated:

| <u>do</u> | [cu] | ***mo tavla*** | <u>mi</u> | [vau] |

You are _____(what?)-kind-of talker to me?

| <u>do</u> | [cu] | ***tavla mo*** | <u>mi</u> | [vau] |

You are talker-wise _____(what?) to me?

As was stated above, you can use scalar negation (na'e and its equivalents) in *tanru*:

| <u>do</u> | [cu] | ***na'e sutra tavla*** | <u>mi</u> | [vau] |

You are an other-than-quick talker (or) *You are a slow talker.*

| <u>do</u> | [cu] | ***sutra na'e tavla*** | <u>mi</u> | [vau] |

You are quickly other-than-talking (or) *You are doing something other-than-talking, quickly.*

Quantified *selbri* ("*number* moi")

Lojban numbers are expressed as strings of digits. The basic digits are:

pa	re	ci	vo	mu	xa	ze	bi	so	no	pi
1	2	3	4	5	6	7	8	9	0	.

number moi (usually combined into one word) (**ordinal numbers**):

| <u>le tavla [ku]</u> | | cu | ***ci moi*** | [vau] |

The talker is third.

number mei (usually combined into one word) (**cardinal numbers**):

<u>le tavla ku</u>   [cu] *ci mei*   [vau]
The talkers are a-threesome.

number si'e (usually combined into one word) (**portional numbers**):

<u>le blari'o ku</u>   [cu] *pimu si'e*   [vau]
The blue-green (things) are a .5 portion (a half).

number cu'o (usually combined into one word) (**probability numbers**):

<u>le blari'o ku</u>   [cu] *pimu cu'o*   [vau]
The blue-green (occurrences) are a .5 probability (have a 50% chance).

Note the interpretation of x_1 in the last example, which is a result of the place structure of probability numbers. Each of these special kinds of *selbri* have other places besides the x_1 *sumti* that appear in these examples.

 Number *selbri* may also be used as part of a *tanru*:

<u>mi</u>   [cu] *papa moi tavla*   <u>do</u>   [vau]
I am the 11th talker to you.

The place structure again is that of the final component of the *tanru*.

Attaching internal *sumti* to a *selbri*

Each component of a *tanru* is not merely a single-word *brivla*, but a representation of an entire *bridi* relationship. Lojban grammar allows the *sumti* that complete and define that *bridi* to be incorporated into the *selbri*. Combined *sumti* are called **internal *sumti***. We'll first show the structure of such a complex *selbri* component:

 brivla/selbri be <u>sumti</u> [bei <u>sumti</u>] [bei <u>sumti</u>] ... [bei <u>sumti</u>] [be'o]

where the *sumti* attached with be is normally x_2, and other *sumti* are optionally attached in numerical order (x_3, x_4, x_5), each preceded by the marker bei. be'o is the end-marker for internal *sumti*, appearing after the last internal *sumti* for a *brivla* or other *selbri*. Let's now look at one way that this construct is used.

tanru with internal *sumti*

Using the internal *sumti* structure, any of the components of a *tanru* can have its own *sumti*:

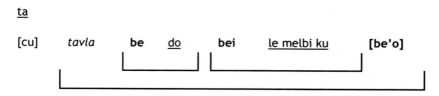

vecnu [vau]
That is a talker–to-you–about-the-beautiful-thing(s) salesperson (or, more simply) *That's a salesperson who talks to you about beautiful things.*

In compound constructs such as this one, the normally **elidable** (omissible) right terminators may be mandatory to keep the sentence unambiguous. Thus, in this last example, either the ku or the be'o must not be elided (ku was chosen arbitrarily). Otherwise, vecnu is absorbed into the internal *sumti*:

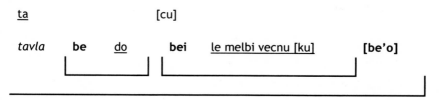

[vau]
That is a talker-to-you-about-the-beautiful-salesperson (or) *That one talks about beautiful salespeople to you.*

Obviously, a different statement. In Lojban, you *must* be careful about properly including terminators when needed. If in doubt, include the terminator; the statement *cannot* be ambiguous with the terminator present.

In the last example, by omitting the elidable terminators ku and be'o, we ended up with *sumti* attached to the *selbri* word in final position. The latter sentence is thus identical in meaning to the same sentence expressed without internal *sumti*:

<u>ta</u>   [cu]   *tavla*   <u>do</u>   <u>le melbi vecnu [ku] [vau]</u>
That is a talker-to-you-about-the-beautiful-salesperson (or) *That one talks about beautiful salespeople to you.*

Internal *sumti* can use any *sumti* construct, including the fa/fe/fi/fo/fu series to rearrange place orders:

<u>ta</u>   [cu]   *tavla*   be <u>do</u>   bei fo <u>la lojban.</u>   [be'o]

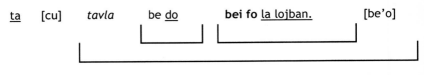

vecnu   [vau]
That is a talker-to-you-in-Lojban salesperson (or, more simply) *That's a salesperson who talks to you in Lojban.*

tanru inversion ("modified-*selbri* co modifier-*selbri*")

We rephrased the English translations of the Lojban in the last two examples in order to simplify the English structure and make the sentence more clear. The same type of rearrangement is possible in Lojban. The technique is called *tanru* **inversion**. The modifier *selbri* is placed *after* the modified one, with a co separating them:

modified-*selbri* co modifier-*selbri*

The co can often be translated as 'of type'.

tanru inversion affects the interpretation of *sumti* that are in the surrounding *bridi* relationship. The inversion causes a new *brivla* to be in the final position, and any following *sumti* are associated with that final *brivla* of the modifier-*selbri*. The *sumti* *preceding* the *selbri* are still associated with the final term of the modified-*selbri*, because that is the primary relation being claimed by the sentence. So, in this case *sumti* belong to the *selbri* they are closest to.

One obvious advantage of *tanru* inversion is to simplify the apparent structure of a *selbri*. As we have said, the final *selbri* in a *tanru* does not need to use internal *sumti* structures in order to attach its *sumti*. The first of the examples above that use internal *sumti* thus becomes the simpler:

<u>ta</u> [cu] *vecnu*   co   *tavla* <u>do</u> <u>le melbi [ku]</u> [vau]
That is a seller of-type talker to you about the beautiful thing(s) (or) That's a salesperson who talks to you about beautiful things.

do and le melbi [ku] are the x_2 and x_3 places of tavla, while ta remains the x_1 of the underlying modified-relation, which is vecnu.

The resulting Lojban now matches the colloquial English phrasing more closely, and the sentence is simpler since it does not require the complex marker system needed for internal *sumti*.

All of the forms of *selbri* listed in this section are governed by rules that form a hierarchy. The most complex constructs are those using rules higher in the hierarchy. In general, constructs built from higher rules cannot be used inside lower-rule constructs. This hierarchy of rules is the primary reason why Lojban's grammar is unambiguous.

Inversion of *tanru* uses rules which are highest in the hierarchy, thus allowing you to invert almost all other *selbri* constructs. However, this also means that you *cannot* substitute a *tanru* inversion into most other constructs within a *selbri*.

selbri grouping in *tanru*

tanru may be composed of more than two components, any of which may be more complex than the simple *brivla* and/or other *selbri* structures discussed above. Lojban allows complex *tanru* structures to be unambiguously expressed, so that any such complex structure can be broken down into a series of modifier–modified pairs. We present two of the variety of ways to express more complex groupings.

In the absence of any grouping indications, components in *tanru* are presumed grouped from the left:

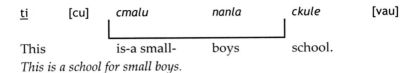

| ti | [cu] | *cmalu* | *nanla* | *ckule* | [vau] |

| This | | is-a small- | boys | school. |

This is a school for small boys.

But what if we want to group this *selbri* so as to talk about a 'boys school' which is small? One way is with *tanru* inversion:

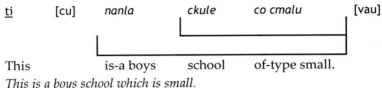

| ti | [cu] | *nanla* | *ckule* | *co cmalu* | [vau] |

| This | | is-a boys | school | of-type small. |

This is a boys school which is small.

tanru inversion can work for many simple grouping problems. However, since it changes the final *brivla*, it affects the interpretation of any *sumti* following the *selbri*. There is a more general solution that does not affect which *selbri* is in final position, a choice that might be important because of the structural markers required.

Any *selbri*, or any portion of a *tanru* that could stand alone as a *selbri*, may be surrounded with word-brackets ke (left) and ke'e (right) to indicate priority in grouping. Normally, you will only use ke/ke'e grouping around strings of two or more *selbri* components, since the structure conveys no useful grouping information around a single *selbri*. At the end of the *selbri*, and in other places where no ambiguity results, the ke'e terminator becomes optional (elidable):

| ti | [cu] |
| This | |

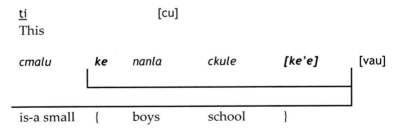

| *cmalu* | *ke* | *nanla* | *ckule* | *[ke'e]* | [vau] |

| is-a small | { | boys | school | } |

A *selbri* structure surrounded by ke and ke'e has the same grammar as a single word *brivla*. As a result, you can modify such structures with na'e and other scalar negation words, or with se and other conversion words:

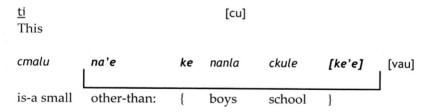

| <u>ti</u> | | | | [cu] | | |
| This | | | | | | |

cmalu	*na'e*	*ke*	*nanla*	*ckule*	*[ke'e]*	[vau]
is-a small	other-than:	{	boys	school	}	

Abstraction *selbri*

The final *selbri* form we cover here isn't found very often in *selbri* in their most basic form. However, it turns out to be one of the most important constructs in the language, showing up frequently as a part of more complex structures. This *selbri* form is called **sentence abstraction**. The basic form is:

nu-word complete-*bridi*-sentence [kei]

where the *bridi* sentence inside the two markers can be a Lojban sentence of *any* type discussed here, no matter how complex. The word nu indicates an **event abstraction**, the most common kind of abstraction found in Lojban.

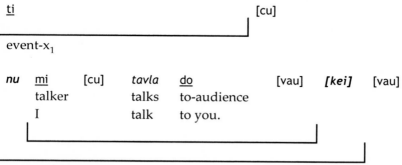

| <u>ti</u> | | | | [cu] |
| event-x_1 | | | | |

nu	<u>mi</u>	[cu]	*tavla*	<u>do</u>	[vau]	*[kei]*	[vau]
	talker		talks	to-audience			
	I		talk	to you.			

event-of "I talk to you."
This is an event of my talking to you.

The term *event* should not be misconstrued. In Lojban, it can refer to a momentary occurrence, or to a situation lasting hours, days, or even an indefinite period of time. nu can stand for any of these kinds and durations of events. Other words may substitute for nu when you need to be specific and indicate particular **event contours**, such as a **point event** in time (mu'e) or a steady, unchanging **state** (za'i) of indefinite duration.

There are other types of abstractions, as well, each indicated by words that substitute for nu. The most common of these are ka for a property/quality abstraction and du'u for a fact/assertion abstraction. These will be exemplified in the next section. Most abstraction *selbri* have only one place (x_1) which is the event, property, fact or other abstract 'thing' being described by the *selbri*.

Abstractions, like other *selbri*, may be used in *tanru*; indeed, they are more common in *tanru* than alone:

<u>ti</u>   [cu]   *sutra bajra cukta*   [vau]
This is-a fast-runner book.

which might be a book about fast runners, while:

<u>ti</u> [cu]   *sutra*   **nu** *bajra*   **kei**   *cukta*   [vau]

This is-a fast-event(s)-of-running book.

which is more likely a book about races, or a how-to book about running fast. Note that the kei could not be elided in the last example, or the following would have resulted:

<u>ti</u> [cu]   *sutra*   **nu** *bajra*   *cukta*   **[kei]**   [vau]

This is-a fast event-of runner-book.

and one imagines a very short-lived book about runners (it is the *event* that is fast, not the running or the book).

Most abstractions that appear often in *selbri* like this tend to be abbreviated into a single-word *selbri* (a *brivla*) which embeds the nu into the concept. Such compounds don't require a kei, since the abstraction encompasses only the idea expressed within the single word. Lojban compound words (*lujvo*) are composed of combining forms of their component *brivla* (content words like bajra) and **cmavo** (short structure words like nu).

   The rules for constructing *lujvo* are not difficult if you have a list of the combining forms (called **rafsi**); the rules are designed carefully to ensure that the pieces stay attached together and cannot be accidentally interpreted as separate words. This is because (as in the last example) the grammar of separate words may require added markers and terminators to obtain the meaning that you intend. The *lujvo* for an event of running is formed from nun, the *rafsi* combining form of nu, and bajra, which serves as its own combining form:

sumti	nunbajra	sumti	sumti	sumti	sumti
event	[running]	runner	on-surface	using-limbs	with-gait

x_1 *is an event of* x_2 *running on surface* x_3 *using limbs* x_4, *with gait* x_5.

Comparing this place structure with the one at the beginning of this section, you will see that x_1 has been assigned to the event, while the remaining places are those of bajra. With this new *lujvo*, the next to the last example sentence:

<u>ti</u>	[cu]	*sutra*	*nu*	*bajra*	*kei*	*cukta*	[vau]

This is-a fast-events-of-running book.

can be reformulated as the less complicated structure:

<u>ti</u>	[cu]	*sutra*	**nunbajra**	*cukta*	[vau]

This is-a fast-events-of-running book.

Complex *sumti*

More le *selbri* [ku] descriptions

Now that we have seen a variety of *selbri* forms, it may become obvious that any of these *selbri* structures can be used in description *sumti* marked with le. Indeed, some of these structures, especially internal *sumti* and abstractions, are much more commonly found embedded in *sumti*, than in the *selbri* defining the main relation of the sentence.

| <u>ko</u> | [cu] | *tavla* | <u>le sutra klama [ku]</u> | | [vau] |

You (imperative) talk to the quick-goer. (Talk to the quick-goer.)

| <u>do</u> | [cu] | *klama* | <u>le se tavla [ku]</u> | <u>ta</u> | [vau] |

You go to the one-talked-to from that.

This last example shows the virtue of se conversion. It has allowed us to mentally convert tavla to make its x_2 place accessible by description in the *sumti*.

Now for a tricky usage. We use go'i to refer to the *bridi* of the last sentence. Therefore le go'i [ku] refers to the first place of that *bridi* (in this case, the go-er, do). If we want to refer to the second place of the last sentence *bridi*, the destination, we can mentally convert that sentence using se: so le se go'i [ku] means the destination (le se klama [ku] = le se tavla [ku]).

| **<u>le se go'i [ku]</u>** | | cu | *melbi* | [vau] |

The destination is beautiful (or) *The one talked-to (the destination) is beautiful.*

| <u>le na'e melbi [ku]</u> | cu | *tavla* | <u>ta</u> | [vau] |

The other-than-beautiful one talks to that one.

| <u>mi</u> | [cu] | *tavla* | <u>le mo klama [ku]</u> | <u>ri</u> | [vau] |

I talk to the what-kind-of go-er about itself?

le re moi prenu [ku]   cu   *tavla*   mi   [vau]
The second person talks to me.

It is *important* to remember and correctly use the elidable separator cu with description *selbri*. If you misplace it or omit it (or its less-often used alternative ku), you will create some very strange *tanru*.

le sutra [ku]   cu   vecnu cukta   [vau]
The quick-one is a seller book.

le sutra vecnu [ku]   cu   cukta   [vau]
The quick seller is a book.

And, if you omit the cu altogether, you get only a *sumti*:

le sutra vecnu cukta [ku]   [vau]
The quick-seller book.

sumti descriptions with internal *sumti*

The phrase

le *selbri*   be *sumti* bei *sumti* bei *sumti* ... bei *sumti* [be'o]   ku

is all one *sumti*:

le tavla   be mi   bei le vecnu [ku] [be'o]   [ku]

The talker   to me   about the seller

cu   *klama*   [vau]
          goes.

You can even fill in the places of an internal *sumti*:

le tavla
The talker

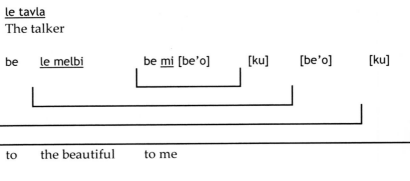

to   the beautiful   to me

cu   *klama* [vau]
                            goes.

The talker to the one who is beautiful to me goes. (The person talking to the one I think is beautiful, goes.)

Without the omitted terminators this looks a bit less wordy:

le tavla be le melbi be mi cu klama
The one talking to the one I think is beautiful, goes.

A *selbri* can consist of a *tanru* with internal *sumti*; therefore a *sumti* may be built on such a *selbri*, possibly even having internal *sumti* on *both* components of a *tanru* . (In a *tanru* embedded within a *sumti*, even the *sumti* attached to the final component must be attached with be/bei/ be'o):

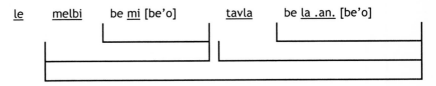

[ku] cu *vecnu* <u>ti</u> [vau]
The beautiful-to-me talker-to-Ann sells this. (The one I think is beautiful who is talking to Ann, sells this.)

Here, either the ku or the cu is elidable before the main *selbri* (both instances of be'o are unconditionally elidable). Most frequently, when there is a choice, the terminator that best communicates the sentence structure is chosen. cu, in this case, clearly separates the complex *sumti* from the *selbri*, and is preferred. Often a single cu may allow you to omit several elidable terminators that would otherwise be necessary. This happens most frequently with abstraction *selbri* that are used in *sumti* descriptions.

Abstraction *sumti* clauses

Abstraction *sumti* clauses take the form "le nu sentence kei":

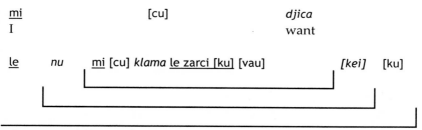

the event-of: I go to the store

[vau]
I want to go to the store.

With the elidable terminators not printed, this sentence looks much shorter:

mi djica le nu mi klama le zarci
I want to go to the store.

An even shorter form will typically appear in Lojban text. le nu occurs so frequently in combination that it is often written as a single word. This isn't mandatory—*cmavo* compounds are always understood as meaning the same thing as the words written separately. *cmavo* are generally written as one word when they together equate to a concept that is written in other languages as one word.

In addition, the mi inside the abstraction will often be omitted. When a listener hears this sentence and realizes that the go-er wasn't specified, the obvious value(s) will be assumed (as with the origin, the route and the means). Leaving out the mi is exactly comparable to the difference between the two English sentences:

I want to go to the store (and) *I want myself to go to the store.*

mi djica lenu klama le zarci
I want to go to the store.

If an abstraction is in the x_1 position, cu allows four other elidable markers to be omitted. An example is the following conversion of the last example sentence:

<u>le</u>   *nu* <u>mi</u> [cu] *klama* <u>le zarci [ku]</u> **[vau] [kei]**   **[ku]**

cu *se djica* <u>mi</u> [vau]
The-event-of: (I go to the store) is desirable to me.

Using cu makes things much easier for the listener, who thus knows in one word that the complex *sumti* is completely ended and the main *selbri* comes next.

We promised to give examples of two of the other types of abstractions in this section. These abstractions tend to be associated with specific places of particular *brivla*.

<u>la mark.</u>   [cu]   *ricfu*   <u>le **ka** melbi [vau] [kei] [ku]</u>
Mark is rich in the quality of x_1 being beautiful to x_2 by standard x_3.

<u>mi</u>   [cu]   *djuno*
I   know

<u>le **du'u** la djan.</u> [cu] te vecnu [vau] [kei] [ku]   [vau]
the-fact-that John is a buyer.
I know that John buys (something).

As with the earlier examples, these sentences will typically appear much shorter in print:

la mark. ricfu leka melbi
Mark is rich in beauty.

mi djuno ledu'u la djan. te vecnu
I know that John buys (something).

Quantified *sumti* ("le number [boi] *selbri* [ku]")

One way to quantify a *sumti* being described is to insert the number followed by a terminator boi, which may be omitted when no ambiguity results (the usual case):

le **re [boi]** tavla [ku] cu *klama* [vau]
The two talkers go.

boi may not be elided when a number *selbri* follows, since you wouldn't know otherwise where one number stops and the next begins (Lojban does not allow such boundaries to be expressed by contrastive stress as in English):

le reno **boi** remei [ku] cu *klama* [vau]
The twenty twosomes (pairs) go.

Quantified selection from *sumti* ("number [boi] le [number] [boi] *selbri* [ku]")

You can also put a number preceding the le, to select from the set of individuals indicated by the description:

re [boi]	le tavla [ku]	cu	*klama*	[vau]
2...				

Two of the (unspecified number of) talkers go.

re [boi]	le reno boi remei [ku]	cu	*klama*	[vau]
2...				

Two of the twenty twosomes go. (i.e. four altogether)

le tavla	be	pa [boi]	le ci [boi] bajra [ku]	[be'o]
(begin)		1...		
The talker	to	one of	the three runners	

[ku]	cu	*melbi* [vau]
(end)		is-beautiful

Indefinite description *sumti* ("lo *selbri* [ku]")

If you wish to describe a *sumti*, but do not have a specific instance of the *sumti* in mind, you can instead refer generically to something that meets the terms of the description *selbri*:

lo tavla [ku] cu *klama* [vau]
A talker goes (or) *Some talkers go.*

lo may be used interchangeably with le in the preceding examples, with an **indefinite** description as a result.

Lojban allows you to omit the lo in:

number [boi] [lo] [number [boi]] *selbri* [ku]

re [boi] [lo] tavla [ku] cu *klama* [vau] =
re tavla cu klama
Two [of the unspecified number who are] talkers go.

di'u and la'e di'u

In English, if I say *The school is beautiful,* you might reply *This pleases me.* How do you know what *this* refers to? Lojban uses different expressions to convey the possible meanings of English *this.* So, given the sentence:

le ckule [ku] cu *melbi* [vau]
The school is beautiful.

the following three sentences all might translate as "This pleases me."

ri cu *pluka* mi [vau]
This (the school, the last expressed sumti*) pleases me.*

di'u cu *pluka* **mi** [vau]
This (the last sentence) *pleases me* (perhaps because it is grammatical or sounds nice).

la'e di'u cu *pluka* **mi** [vau]
This (what the last sentence refers to; i.e. that the school is beautiful) *pleases me.*

The last sentence is an example of using one *sumti* to point to or refer to another by inference. la'edi'u is often written as a single word, and is used more often than di'u by itself.

Other *sumti* types

Lojban supports several other *sumti* types, more than we can discuss in a short paper. These include bare numbers, and several kinds of quoted text (single words, grammatical text, potentially ungrammatical text, and non-Lojban text).

Attachments to *sumti*, *selbri* and sentences

Attachments to *sumti*

All structures in this section apply to *sumti* at the main level of a sentence, as well as to *sumti* within substructures.

Adding a new *sumti* place to a *bridi* relationship ("modal + *sumti*")

The modal tags, or *sumti tcita*, specify relationships such as time or location: e.g. pu 'before', ba 'after', ca 'simultaneous with', vi 'at', va 'near', vu 'far from'
    There are many more of these, and some specialized rules for compounding them. These are discussed in the reference grammar.

<u>mi</u>   [cu]   *tavla*

pu   <u>le nu do [cu] tavla [vau] [kei] [ku]</u>   [vau]
PAST _____|
mi tavla pu lenu do tavla
I talk before the-act-of you talk.
I talk before you do.

You must think carefully about what you mean with these constructions:

<u>mi</u>   [cu]   *tavla*   **pu**   <u>do</u>   [vau]
                                   | PAST _____|
I talk before you. (I talked before you even existed.)

Modal tags proper can also be used to add new *sumti* places to a *selbri*:
e.g. secau (without ...), mu'i (motivational because ...), du'o (according to ...)

<u>do</u>   [cu]   *klama*   **secau**   <u>mi</u>   [vau]
                                   | WITHOUT _____|
You go without me.

Modal questions ("modal + ma")

These express common English questions using time, location, and modal tag words combined with ma:

ca <u>ma</u> <u>do</u> [cu] *tavla* [vau]
Simultaneous-with ____(what?), you talk?
When do you talk?

vi <u>ma</u> <u>do</u> [cu] *tavla* [vau]
At ____(what?), you talk?
Where do you talk?

mu'i <u>ma</u> <u>do</u> [cu] *tavla* [vau]
Motivationally-because ____(what?), you talk?
Why do you talk?

(Lojban has other 'because' modal tags for asking a variety of different 'why?' questions.)

sumti relative phrases (*"sumti* pe modifier-*sumti* [ge'u]*"*)

A *sumti* may be identified more exactly by attaching a **relative phrase**, another *sumti*, that in some way restricts the possible set of things being referred to:

le cukta [ku]	pe	le vecnu [ku]	[ge'u]
	OF		

cu   *blari'o*   [vau]
The book of the salesperson is blue-green.

pe, the basic marker of a **restrictive relative phrase**, is vague as to the exact nature of the relationship between the original *sumti* and the *sumti* that it is identifying. It is thus similar to the loosest English possessive, as in *my chair/a chair of mine*, which may for instance be used for a chair that you sit in but which is owned by someone else.

Successively tighter degrees of association/possession are indicated by po (**alienable** possession) and po'e (**inalienable** possession):

le cukta [ku]	po	mi	[ge'u]
	OF		

The book of mine. (Even if you are holding it, it is still my book. But I also could give it to you, making it no longer my book.)

le birka [ku]	po'e	mi	[ge'u]
	OF		

The arm of mine. (It is intrinsically *my* arm; it cannot be given away, even if cut off.)

po'u restricts a *sumti* by giving another *identity*: a *sumti* that could equivalently replace the original:

la djan.	po'u	le vecnu [ku]	[ge'u]
	OF		

John	who-is	the seller

cu	*klama*	[vau]
	goes.	

John-the-salesman goes.

goi, used like pe, defines ko'a and other variable *sumti* for use throughout a text without repeating:

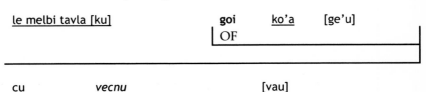

le melbi tavla [ku]		goi	ko'a	[ge'u]
		OF		

cu	*vecnu*	[vau]

The beautiful talker (hereinafter ko'a) *sells.*

.i ko'a *djica* lenu do klama ko'a [vau] [kei] [ku] [vau]
He/she (the beautiful talker) wants the event of you going to him/her.

Lojban has words identical in grammar to pe that provide **non-restrictive** (incidental) information about a *sumti*. ne is the non-restrictive (incidental) equivalent of pe.

This construct may be combined with the modal construct discussed just previously to identify a *sumti*:

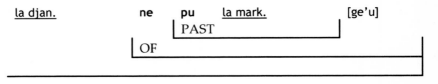

la djan.	ne	pu	la mark.	[ge'u]
		PAST		
	OF			

[cu]	*melbi tavla*	[vau]

John, who was (incidentally) before Mark, is a beautiful-talker.

The contrast between ne (incidental) and pe (identifying) is shown by giving the same sentence with pe:

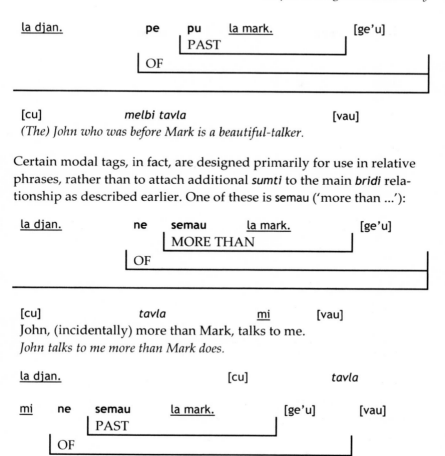

[cu]   *melbi tavla*   [vau]
(The) John who was before Mark is a beautiful-talker.

Certain modal tags, in fact, are designed primarily for use in relative phrases, rather than to attach additional *sumti* to the main *bridi* relationship as described earlier. One of these is semau ('more than ...'):

[cu]   *tavla*   *mi*   [vau]
John, (incidentally) more than Mark, talks to me.
John talks to me more than Mark does.

John talks to me, (incidentally) more than Mark.
John talks to me more than he does to Mark.

Without linking a semau modal *sumti* to another *sumti* with ne or pe, it is hard to understand:

???la djan.	[cu]	*tavla*	mi

semau	la mark.	[vau]
MORE THAN		

John talks to me, more than Mark. (but Mark is bound neither to
John nor me, but to the talking).
(John's talking to me) is more than (Mark).

Comparing a talking relationship to a person is nonsense.

sumti relative clauses ("*sumti* poi sentence ku'o")

pe-phrases are limited to what can be expressed in a single *sumti*.
When you need to include more complete information about a *sumti*,
Lojban provides for **relative clauses**. A **restrictive relative clause
marker**, poi, marks a following complete *bridi* as information that
identifies the *sumti* by providing a relationship that the *sumti* fits into.

The placeholder for the *sumti* being identified is ke'a, which is
merely another in the set of single-word *sumti*. ke'a is often left out if it
is contextually obvious where it would go (especially when ke'a
would go in the x_1 position immediately after poi, or in the first available unspecified place if x_1 is already filled). A relative clause is
terminated with the marker ku'o, which may be omitted if no ambiguity will result. It is very rare that ku'o needs to be expressed overtly.

le ckule [ku]
The school

poi	mi	[cu]	*klama*	ke'a	[vau]	[ku'o]
REL						
which	I		go-to	it		

cu	*blari'o*	[vau]
	is-blue-green	

The school I go to is blue-green.

Note that ke'a refers to the school.

le bajra [ku]	poi	[ke'a] [cu] *tavla* [vau] [ku'o]
	REL	

cu	vecnu	[vau]

le bajra poi tavla cu vecnu
The runner who talks is a seller.

There is also a **non-restrictive relative clause** marker, noi, for incidental information about a *sumti*.

Tensed *sumti* ("le time/location/modal-tag + *selbri* [ku]")

A *sumti* may also have a time or location or modal tag placed in front of its description *selbri*:

le **pu** bajra [ku] cu *tavla* [vau]
The earlier/former/past runner talked/talks. (Since Lojban tense is optional, we don't know when she talked—but we do know when she ran.)

le **vi** bajra [ku] cu *tavla* [vau]
The here runner talks.
This runner talks.

Short possessive *sumti* ("le possessor-*sumti* *selbri* [ku]")

A description *sumti* can also have a *sumti* after the le but before the *selbri*, resulting in an abbreviated form of the loose pe possessive:

le **ti** bajra [ku] [cu] *tavla* [vau]
The this-one's runner talked/talks.
This one's runner talks.

This sentence is completely equivalent to:

<u>le bajra [ku]</u> pe <u>ti</u> [cu] *tavla* [vau]
The runner of this-one talked/talks.
This one's runner talks.

A more complete structure of a **description** *sumti* is "[number] le [number] [*sumti*] [modal] *selbri* [ku]".

Attachments to *selbri*

Tensed or adverbial *bridi* relationships

Immediately after cu and before a *selbri*, you can have a modal. (The modal being there may make cu redundant, since modals cannot be absorbed into *tanru*, so they cannot be conflated with the *selbri* itself.) Such modals serve as an equivalent to English tenses and adverbs. In Lojban, tense is completely optional. If unspecified, tense is picked up from context.

<u>do</u>   [cu]   **vu**   *vecnu*   <u>zo'e</u>   [vau]
                    | YONDER
You yonder sell something-unspecified.

<u>le vi tavla [ku]</u>   [cu]   **ba**   *klama*   [vau]
                            | FUTURE
The here talker will go.
This talker will go.

<u>do</u>   [cu]   **mu'i**   *tavla*   <u>mi</u>   [vau]
                    | MOTIVE
You motivatedly talk to me (i.e. with a certain purpose in mind).

Attachments to sentences

A variety of constructs may occur anywhere in a sentence, operating independent of the primary grammar of the sentence. These constructs generally have minimal internal grammar. Like xu, when they are not at the beginning of a sentence, they indicate emphasis on the word or construct that they immediately follow.

Attitudinals

Attitudinals include a variety of expressions conveyed in English through interjections or tone of voice. Lojban supports an enormous range of emotional expression through specific words and compounds. Indicators may be modified for intensity, or classified by the sphere that they apply to (social, mental, emotional, physical, sexual, spiritual).

.ie <u>mi</u> [cu] *klama* [vau]
Agreement! I go.
Yep! I'll go.

.ei sai <u>mi</u> [cu] *klama* [vau]
Strong obligation! I go.
I really should go.

<u>mi</u> [cu] *klama* .o'u nai ro'a <u>le ckule</u> [ku] [vau]
I go to the school (and I am socially stressed to be going).

<u>mi</u> [cu] *klama* <u>le ckule</u> .ui [ku] [vau]
I go to the school (and I am happy because it is the school I'm going to).

Discursives

Discursives allow free expression of certain **metalinguistic comments** (comments about the text). Use of discursives allows clear separation of these metalinguistic features from the underlying statements and logical structure. By comparison, the English words *but* and *also*, which discursively indicate contrast or added weight-of-example, are *logically* equivalent to *and* without that discursive content. The average English speaker does not think about, and may not even realize, the contrary-seeming idea that *but* basically means *and*.

<u>mi</u> [cu] *klama* [vau] .i <u>do</u> [cu] *stali* [vau]
I go. You stay.

<u>mi</u> [cu] *klama* [vau] .i ji'a <u>do</u> [cu] *stali* [vau]
I go. In addition, you stay. (added weight)

<u>mi</u> [cu] *klama* [vau] .i ku'i <u>do</u> [cu] *stali* [vau]
I go. However, you stay. (contrast)

Evidentials

Evidentials indicate the speaker's relationship to the statement, specifically communicating what kind of knowledge the speaker is basing the statement on. These include za'a ("I directly observe the relationship"), pe'i ("I opine that the relationship holds") ru'a ("I postulate"), and others. Many Native American languages use these type of words.

pe'i <u>do</u> [cu] *melbi* [vau]
I opine! You are beautiful.

za'a <u>do</u> [cu] *melbi* [vau]
I directly observe! You are beautiful.

Some expressions overlap between categories, behaving as indicators as well as evidentials (.ia, belief, faith), or attitudinals/discursives (ga'i, hauteur, relative high-rank; cf. Japanese).

.e'a ga'i <u>ko'a</u> [cu] *citka* <u>lo titnanba [ku]</u> [vau]
Permission!/I permit! Hauteur! They eat cake.
Let them eat cake!

Logical Connectives

Lojban expresses **logical connectives** so as to unambiguously indicate **logical scope** (the extent of the expressions being connected), as well as to isolate various non-logical features from the logical ones (as noted above for discursives). Logical connectives may be expressed in **forethought** forms, in which the relationship is specified before the two terms (*both ... and ...*); or **afterthought** forms, in which the relationship is specified between the two terms (*..., and ...*). The form of logical connectives directly indicates their scope and the associated **truth table** for the two connected terms. For example, a bare vowel joins *sumti* (.a 'alternation', *a* and/or *b*, *a* OR *b*; .e 'conjunction', *a* AND *b*). na and nai may be used to negate connected terms (na.a 'conditional', not *a* OR *b*, if *a* then *b*; .anai 'conditional', *a* or not *b*, *a* if *b*).

The parallel structures are shown in the following abbreviated table:

	sumti	*sumti* forethought	sentences
OR (*a* and/or *b*)	.a	ga *sumti* gi *sumti*	.i ja
AND (*a* and *b*)	.e	ge *sumti* gi *sumti*	.i je
XOR (*a* or *b*, both)	.onai	go *sumti* ginai *sumti*	.i jonai
⇒ (if *a* then *b*; *a* only if *b*)	na.a	ganai *sumti* gi *sumti*	.i naja
⇐ (*a* if *b*; if *b* then *a*)	.anai	ga *sumti* ginai *sumti*	.i janai

	tanru	*tanru* forethought	compound bridi
OR (*a* and/or *b*)	ja	gu'a *selbri* gi *selbri*	gi'a
AND (*a* and *b*)	je	gu'e *selbri* gi *selbri*	gi'e
XOR (*a* or *b*, not both)	jonai	gu'o *selbri* ginai *selbri*	gi'onai
⇒ (if *a* then *b*; *a* only if *b*)	naja	gu'anai *selbri* gi *selbri*	nagi'a
⇐ (*a* if *b*)	janai	gu'a *selbri* ginai *selbri*	gi'anai

These structures are illustrated in the following; as you can see, Lojban can express quite subtle logical distinctions succinctly.

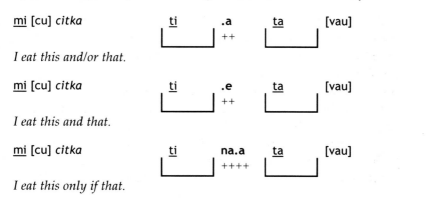

<u>mi</u> [cu] *citka*   <u>ti</u>   .a   <u>ta</u>   [vau]
                                    ++

I eat this and/or that.

<u>mi</u> [cu] *citka*   <u>ti</u>   .e   <u>ta</u>   [vau]
                                    ++

I eat this and that.

<u>mi</u> [cu] *citka*   <u>ti</u>   na.a   <u>ta</u>   [vau]
                                    ++++

I eat this only if that.

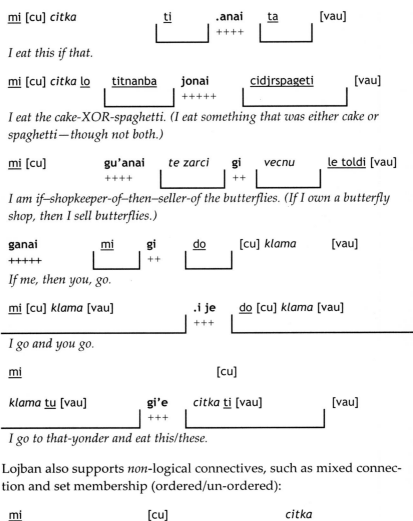

<u>mi</u> [cu] *citka*　　　　ti　　.anai　ta　　[vau]
++++

I eat this if that.

<u>mi</u> [cu] *citka* <u>lo</u>　titnanba　**jonai**　cidjrspageti　[vau]
+++++

I eat the cake-XOR-spaghetti. (I eat something that was either cake or spaghetti—though not both.)

<u>mi</u> [cu]　　**gu'anai** *te zarci*　**gi** *vecnu*　le toldi [vau]
++++　　　　　++

I am if–shopkeeper-of–then–seller-of the butterflies. (If I own a butterfly shop, then I sell butterflies.)

ganai　　mi　**gi**　<u>do</u>　[cu] *klama*　[vau]
+++++　　　　　　　++

If me, then you, go.

<u>mi</u> [cu] *klama* [vau]　　　.i je　<u>do</u> [cu] *klama* [vau]
+++

I go and you go.

<u>mi</u>　　　　　　　　　　[cu]

klama <u>tu</u> [vau]　　**gi'e** *citka* <u>ti</u> [vau]　　[vau]
+++

I go to that-yonder and eat this/these.

Lojban also supports *non*-logical connectives, such as mixed connection and set membership (ordered/un-ordered):

<u>mi</u>　　　　　　[cu]　　　　　　*citka*

<u>le</u>　blari'o　　**joi**　pelxu　　[ku]　　[vau]
+++

I eat the blue-green-mixed-with-yellow (stuff).

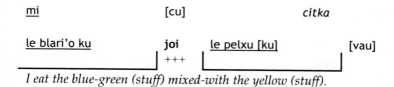

I eat the blue-green (stuff) mixed-with the yellow (stuff).

(The ku before the joi in the latter example *cannot* be left out due to the ambiguity resolution rules invoked in the definition of Lojban.)

Brief glossary of Lojban words used in these examples

cmavo

.a	and/or: *sumti*
.anai	only if: *sumti*
ba	after/future time
be	internal *sumti* link
be'o	end internal *sumti*
bei	more internal *sumti*
bi	8
boi	end-of-number
ca	same time/present
ci	3
co	*tanru* inversion
cu	*selbri* separator
cu'o	probability *selbri*
di'u	last sentence
do	*sumti*: you
du'o	modal: according to...
du'u	abstraction: fact
.e	AND: *sumti*
.e'a	indicator: permission
.ei	indicator: obligation
fa	x_1 *sumti* next
fa'o	end-of-text
fe	x_2 *sumti* next
fi	x_3 *sumti* next
fo	x_4 *sumti* next
fu	x_5 *sumti* next
ga	and/or: forethought

ga'i	indicator: high rank
ganai	if: forethought
ge'u	end relative phrase
gi	forethought medial connective
gi'e	and: *bridi*
go'i	last *bridi*; too; yes!
goi	*sumti* definition
.i	sentence link
.ia	indicator: belief/faith
.ie	indicator: agreement
ja'a	it is true
je	and: *tanru,* sentences
je'a	scalar positive
ji'a	discursive: also
joi	mixed-with 'and'
ka	abstraction: quality
ke	*tanru* grouping
ke'a	relative clause *sumti*
ke'e	end *tanru* grouping
kei	end abstraction
ko	imperative 'You!'
ko'a	he/she/it—assigned variable
ku	end description *sumti*
ku'i	discursive: but
ku'o	end relative clause
la	name follows
la'e	the referent of
la'edi'u	*bridi* of last sentence
le	description *sumti*; the
ledu'u	the fact that ...
leka	the quality of ...
lenu	the event of ...
lo	description *sumti*; a
ma	*sumti* question
mei	cardinal number *selbri*
mi	I; me; we; us
mo	*selbri* question
moi	ordinal number *selbri*
mu	5
mu'e	abstract.: point event

mu'i	modal: motivational cause
na	contradictory negation
na'e	scalar other-than
na.a	only if: *sumti*
nago'i	last *bridi* false; No!
ne	incidental relative phrase
ni'o	new topic
ni'oni'o	new section
no	0; none
no'e	scalar neutral
noi	incidental relative clause
nu	abstraction: event
pa	1
papa	11
pe	identifying phrase
pe'i	evidential: I opine!
pi	decimal point
pimu	.5
po	alienable possession
po'e	inalienable possession
po'u	identity phrase
poi	identifying clause
pu	before/past tense
re	2
remei	twosome, pair
reno	20
ri	the last *sumti*
ru'a	evidential: I assume!
se	x_1/x_2 conversion
secau	modal tag: without...
semau	modal tag: more than
si'e	portion number *selbri*
so	9
ta	that-there; those
te	x_1/x_3 conversion
ti	this-here; these
to'e	scalar opposite
tu	that/those yonder
.ui	indicator: happiness

va	location: near
vau	end of *sumti* list
ve	x_1/x_4 conversion
vi	location: here/at
vo	4
vu	location: far from
xa	6
xe	x_1/x_5 conversion
xu	Is it true?
za'a	evidential: observed
za'i	abstraction: state
ze	7
zo'e	unspecified *sumti*

cmene

.an.	name: Ann
lojban.	name: Lojban
mark.	name: Mark
meris.	name: Mary
tam.	name: Tom

brivla

bajra	x_1 runs on surface x_2 using limbs x_3 with gait x_4
birka	x_1 is a/the arm [body-part] of x_2
blari'o	x_1 is blue-green (color adjective)
bridi	x_1 (text) is a predicate relationship with relation x_2 among arguments (sequence/set) x_3
brivla	x_1 is a word: relation x_2, place structure x_3, language x_4
cidjrspageti	x_1 is a quantity of/contains spaghetti, composition x_2
citka	x_1 eats/ingests/consumes (transitive verb) x_2
ckule	x_1 is school/institute/academy at x_2 teaching subject(s) x_3 to audience/community x_4 operated by x_5
cmalu	x_1 is small in property/dimension(s) x_2 (ka) as compared with standard/norm x_3
cmavo	x_1 is a structure word of grammatical class x_2, with meaning/function x_3 in usage (language) x_4
cukta	x_1 is a book containing work x_2 by author x_3 for audience x_4 preserved in medium x_5

djica	x_1 desires/wants/wishes x_2 (event/state) for purpose x_3
djuno	x_1 knows fact(s) x_2 (du'u) about subject x_3 by epistemology x_4
fu'ivla	x_1 is a loanword meaning x_2 in language x_3 copied from source word x_4
gismu	x_1 is a (Lojban) root word expressing relation x_2 among argument roles x_3, with affix(es) x_4
jikca	x_1 interacts/behaves socially with x_2; x_1 socializes with/is sociable towards x_2
klama	x_1 comes/goes to x_2 from x_3 via x_4 using means x_5
lujvo	x_1 (text) is a compound predicate word with meaning x_2 and arguments x_3 built from metaphor x_4
melbi	x_1 is beautiful/pleasant to x_2 in aspect x_3 (ka) by aesthetic standard x_4
nanla	x_1 is a boy/lad [young male person] of age x_2 immature by standard x_3
nunbajra	x_1 event of x_2 runs on surface x_3, limbs x_4, gait x_5
pelxu	x_1 is yellow/golden [color adjective]
pluka	x_1 (event/state) seems pleasant to/pleases x_2 under conditions x_3
prenu	x_1 is a person/people (noun) [not necessarily human]; x_1 displays personality/a persona
rafsi	x_1 is an affix/suffix/prefix/combining-form for word/concept x_2, form/properties x_3, language x_4
ricfu	x_1 is rich/wealthy in goods/possessions/property/aspect x_2
selbri	x_1 is the relation among arguments (sequence/set) x_3 in the predicate relationship given by the text x_2
stali	x_1 remains/stays at/abides/lasts with x_2
sumti	x_1 is a/the argument of predicate/function x_2 filling place x_3 (kind/number)
sutra	x_1 is fast/swift/quick/hastes/rapid at doing/being/bringing about x_2 (event/state)
tanru	x_1 is a binary metaphor formed with x_2 modifying x_3, giving meaning x_4 in usage/instance x_5
tavla	x_1 talks/speaks to x_2 about subject x_3 in language x_4
titnanba	x_1 is sweet-bread/cake made from grains/raw material x_2

toldi	x_1 is a butterfly/moth of species/breed x_2
vecnu	x_1 [seller] sells/vends x_2 [goods/service/commodity] to buyer x_3 for amount/cost/expense x_4
zarci	x_1 is a market/store/exchange/shop(s) selling/trading (for) x_2, operated by/with participants x_3

Chapter 4. Linguistic Issues pertaining to Lojban

bauske se casnu sera'a le lojbo

1. What is the Sapir–Whorf hypothesis?

The Sapir–Whorf hypothesis is the notion that the language you speak affects the way you think. Most people who have learnt a foreign language, or have grown up speaking two languages, will be familiar with this idea, having found themselves thinking and speaking in one language or the other because something is easier to say in that language. One of the main ideas behind the Loglan/Lojban project was to create a language which is both highly expressive and as culturally neutral as possible, then see what people from different cultures do with it.

To give an example, in most European languages tense and gender are very important, and need to be made explicit in most utterances — you can say "She goes", "It went", "He'll go" and so on; but just to say "She/he/it go", with no particular gender or time in mind, sounds strange. In Chinese, on the other hand, *tā qù* ('he/she/it go') is perfectly normal. In Lojban there are plenty of words to show the time of an action, its length, how it happens and so on — but you don't have to use any of them. If you really wanted to, you could say:

le ninmu puzuze'udi'i klama
the female-human past-long-time-distance-long-time-interval-
regularly go
A long time ago, for a long time, she went regularly.

But you can equally well say:

klama
[someone/something] go

Notice that you can translate the first example into English (more-or-less) but the second one just won't go into English, or most European languages. If you speak a European language and this strikes you as odd, you may have just witnessed a Sapir–Whorf effect! Understanding the potential for Sapir–Whorf effects may lead to better intercultural understanding, promoting communication and peace.

It is known that people's ideas and thought change somewhat when they learn a foreign language. It is not known whether this change is due to exposure to a different culture, or even just getting outside of one's own culture. It is also not known how much (if any) of the change is due to the nature of the language, as opposed to the cultural associations.

The Sapir–Whorf hypothesis was important in linguistics in the 1950s, but interest fell off afterwards, partially because testing it properly was so difficult. Lojban allows a new approach to such testing. Obviously, if a culture-independent language could be taught to groups of people, the effects of language could more easily be separated from those of culture.

Unique features of Lojban remove constraints on language in the areas of logic, ambiguity, and expressive power, opening up areas of thought that have not been easily accessible to human language before. Meanwhile, the formal rigidity of the language definition allows speakers to carefully control their expressions (and perhaps therefore their thought processes). This gives some measure of predictive power that can be used in designing and preparing for actual Sapir–Whorf experiments.

One of the prerequisites of a Sapir–Whorf experiment is an international body of Lojban speakers. We need to be able to teach Lojban to subjects who know only their native (non-English) tongue, and we need to know in advance the difficulties that people from each language and culture will have in learning Lojban. Thus, the Lojban community is actively reaching out to speakers of languages other than English.

Lojban does not need to prove or disprove the Sapir–Whorf hypothesis in order to be successful. However, if evidence is produced supporting the Sapir–Whorf effect, Lojban will likely be perceived as an outstanding tool of analytical and creative thought.

2. Lojban sentences do not have unique interpretations; how can Lojban be said to be unambiguous?
The sense in which Lojban is said to be unambiguous is not a simple one, and some amplification of the basic claim is necessary. Ambiguity can be judged on four levels: the phonological–graphical, the morphological, the syntactic, and the semantic.

Lojban is audio-visually isomorphic: the writing system has a grapheme for every phoneme and vice versa, and there are no suprasegmental phonemes (such as tones or pitch) which are not represented in the writing system. Lojban's phonology contains significant pauses that affect word boundaries, and allows pauses between any two words. The optional written representation for pause is a period, although required pauses can be unambiguously identified in written text from the morphological rules alone. Lojban also uses stress significantly, and again there is a written representation (capitalization of the affected vowel or syllable), which is omitted in most text, where the morphological default of penultimate stress applies.

Lojban is morphologically unambiguous in two senses: a string of phonemes (including explicit pause and stress information) can be broken up into words in only one way, and each compound word can be converted to and from its constituents in only one way.

The syntactic unambiguity of Lojban has been established by the use of a LALR(1) parser generator which, given a series of simple pre-parser operations, produces a unique parse for every Lojban text that follows its grammatical norms. In addition, the existence of a defined 'phrase structure rule' grammar underlying the language (and tested via the parser generator) guarantees that there are no sentences where distinct deep structures generate isomorphic surface structures.

The claim for semantic unambiguity is a limited one only. Lojban contains several constructs which are explicitly ambiguous semantically. The most important of these are Lojban *tanru* (so-called 'metaphors') and Lojban names. Names are ambiguous in almost any language, and Lojban is no better; a name simply must be resolved in context, and the only final authority for the meaning of a name is the user of the name. *tanru* are further discussed in later questions. However, the semantics of the root predicates of Lojban (*gismu*), and of its function words (*cmavo*), are explicitly defined, with a unique, though at times broad, sense.

3. If the meaning of a particular *tanru* cannot be completely understood from understanding the component parts, a separate dictionary entry is needed for every possible *tanru*, making the Lojban dictionary infinitely long. How can this be avoided?

tanru are binary combinations of predicates, such that the second predicate is the 'head' and the first predicate is a modifier for that head. The meaning of the *tanru* is the meaning of its head, with the additional information that there is some unspecified relationship between the head and the modifier.

tanru are the basis of compound words in Lojban. However, a compound word has a single defined meaning whereas the meaning of a *tanru* is explicitly ambiguous. Lojban *tanru* are not as free as English figures of speech; they are 'analytic', meaning that the components of the *tanru* do not themselves assume a figurative sense. Only the connection between them is unstated.

Most of the constructs of Lojban are semantically unambiguous, and there are semantically unambiguous ways (such as with relative clauses) to paraphrase the meaning of any *tanru*. For example, slasi mlatu ('plastic-cat') might be paraphrased in ways that translate to 'cat that is made from plastic' or 'cat which eats plastic' or various other interpretations, just as in English. However, the single (compound) word derived from this *tanru*, slasymlatu, has exactly one meaning from among the interpretations, which could be looked up in a dictionary (if someone had found the word useful enough to formally submit it for inclusion). There is no law compelling the creation of such a word, however, and there is even an 'escape mechanism' allowing a speaker to indicate that a particular instance of a 'nonce' compound word is 'non-standard' (has not been checked against a dictionary or other standard), and may have a meaning based on an unusual interpretation of the underlying *tanru*.

4. The Lojban *gismu* seem to have been chosen at random, without regard to any sort of semantic theory. Why was this done?

Lojban content words are built up from a list of around 1350 root words (*gismu*), which are not necessarily to be taken as semantically simple themselves. Lojban does not claim to exhibit a complete and comprehensive semantic theory which hierarchically partitions the entire semantic space of human discourse. Furthermore, while some *gismu* were chosen because they seem to be semantic primitives, many others (e.g. nanmu, meaning 'human male') are plainly not.

Rather, the 1350-odd root words blanket semantic space, in the sense that everything human beings talk about can be built up using appropriate *tanru*. This claim is being tested in actual usage, and root words can still be added if necessary (after careful consideration), if genuine gaps are found. For the most part, the few gaps which have been recognized (about 20 words have been added in the past decade) reflect the completing of semantic sets. It is no longer permitted for language users to create new *gismu* root words (in the standard form of the language, at least); newly coined words must fall recognizably outside the highly regulated *gismu* morphological space. (A specific and separate morphological structure is reserved for coined words — usually borrowings; and a marker is available to indicate that a word is a 'nonce' coinage rather than an established 'dictionary word').

Lojban's empirically derived word list is similar to that of Basic English, which replaces the whole English vocabulary with English-normal compounds built from about 800 root words. Lojban and Basic English both allow for the adoption of technical terms from other languages to cover things like plant and animal names, food names, and names of chemical compounds.

5. *tanru* like nixli ckule, analogous to English *girls' school*, are so open-ended in sense that there is no way to block such far-fetched interpretations as 'a school intended to train girls between the ages of 6 and 10 to play the bassoon', which is patently absurd. What is the proper interpretation of *tanru*?

The Lojban *tanru* nixli ckule ('girl type of school') cannot mean, out of context, 'school intended to train girls between 6 and 10 years of age to play the bassoon', although if such a school existed it could certainly be called a nixli ckule. This interpretation can be rejected as implausible because it involves additional restrictive information. The undefined relationship between nixli and ckule cannot drag in additional information 'by the hair', as it were. Instead, this intricate interpretation would require a larger *tanru* incorporating nixli ckule as one of its components, or else a non-*tanru* construct, probably involving a Lojban relative clause. By way of comparison, such interpretations as 'school containing girls', 'school whose students are girls', and 'school to train persons to behave like girls' are plausible with minimal context, because these renderings do not involve additional restriction.

6. Lojban claims to be unambiguous, but many constructs have vague meanings, and the meanings of the *gismu* themselves are quite sparsely specified. On the other hand, Lojban forces precision on speakers where it is not wanted and where natural-language speakers can easily avoid it. Is this appropriate to a culturally neutral, unambiguous language?

Lojban's avoidance of ambiguity does not mean an avoidance of vagueness. A Lojban aphorism states that the price of infinite precision is infinite verbosity, as indeed Wilkins' Philosophical Language (1668) illustrates. Lojban's allowable vagueness permits useful sentences to be not much longer than their natural-language counterparts.

There are many ways to omit information in Lojban, and it is up to the listener to reconstruct what was meant, just as in natural languages. In each construct, there are specific required and optional components. Unlike English, omitting an optional component explicitly and unambiguously flags an ellipsis. Furthermore, the listener has a clear way of querying any of this elliptically omitted information.

There are also some categories which are necessary in Lojban and not in other languages. For example, Lojban requires the speaker, whenever referring to objects, to specify whether the objects are considered as individuals, as a mass, or as a (set theoretic) set.

Likewise, logical relations are made explicit: there can be no neutrality in Lojban about inclusive vs. exclusive *or*, which are no more closely related semantically than any other pair of logical connectives.

These properties are a product of Lojban's fundamental design, which was chosen to emphasize a highly distinctive and non-natural syntax (that of formal first-order predicate logic) embedded in a language with the same expressive power as natural languages. Through the appearance of this one highly unusual feature, the intent of the Loglan/Lojban Project has been to maximize one difference between Lojban and natural languages without compromising speakability and learnability. This difference could then be investigated by considering whether the use of first-order predicate logic as a syntactic base has aided fluent Lojban speakers in the use of this logic as a reasoning tool.

Lojban *gismu* roots are defined rather abstractly, in order to cover as large a segment of closely related semantic space as possible. These broad (but not really vague) concepts can then be restricted using *tanru* and other constructs to any arbitrary degree necessary for clarity. Communicating the meaning of a *gismu* (or any other Lojban word) is a problem of teaching and lexicography. The concepts are defined as predicate relationships among various arguments, and various experimental approaches have been explored to determine the best methods of conveying these meanings.

7. Why are Lojban *tanru* involving more than two components always left-grouping (in the absence of a marker word), when right-grouping structure is much more natural to human languages?

Lojban is predominantly a left-grouping language. By default, all structures are left-grouping, with right-grouping available when marked by a particle. Since the head of most constructs appears on the left, left-grouping structures tend to favor the speaker. Nothing spoken needs to be revised to add more information. When the head is on the right, as in the case of *tanru*, left-grouping may seem counter-intuitive, as it requires the listener to retain the entire structure in mind until the head is found. However, left-grouping was retained even in *tanru* for the sake of simplicity.

Experience has shown, however, that Lojban's left-grouping structure is not a major problem for language learners. Indeed, many longer English metaphors translate directly into Lojban using simple left-grouping structures.

8. Why are there so many *cmavo*, and why are many of them so similar? Wouldn't this make Lojban hard to understand at a cocktail party (or a similar noisy environment)?

One of the recurrent difficulties with all forms of Loglan, including Lojban, is the tendency to fill up the available space of structure words, making words of similar function hard to distinguish in noisy environments. This has happened because of the concern that Lojban allow the speaker to be as precise as they choose to be in using Lojban grammar, without privileging one language group's choices of what to express grammatically over another's. The phonological revisions made when Lojban split from Institute Loglan allowed for many more structure words, but once again the list has almost entirely filled.

In some cases, notably the digits 0–9, an effort has been made to separate them phonologically. The vocatives (including the words used for communication protocol, e.g. over the radio) are also maximally separated phonologically. Many other *cmavo* are based on shortened forms of corresponding *gismu* roots, however, and are not maximally separated.

A variety of ways to say "Huh?" have been added to the language, partially alleviating the difficulty. These question words can be used to specify the type of word that was expected, or the part of the relationship that was not understood by the listener.

9. Does Lojban have transformations, as are commonly assumed to exist for natural languages?

Yes, in the sense that there are several alternative surface structures that have the same semantics and therefore, presumably, the same deep structure. What Lojban does not have is identical surface structures with differing deep structures (leading to syntactic ambiguity), so a surface-structure–only grammar is sufficient to

develop an adequate parsing for every text. Knowledge of transformations is required only to get the semantics right.

10. Lojban connectives cannot be used to correctly translate English
If you water it, it will grow, **because material implication is too**
weak and the special causal connectives, which connect assertions,
are too strong. What can be done instead?

The English sentence *If you water it, it will grow* looks superficially
like a Lojban na.a connection (material implication), but it actually has
causal connotations not present in na.a. Therefore, a proper translation
must involve the notion of cause. Neither the Lojban coordinating
causal conjunction nor the two correlative subordinating causal conjunctions (one of which subordinates the cause and the other the
effect) will serve, since these require that either the cause, or the effect,
or both be asserted. Instead, the correct translation of the English
involves 'cause' as a predicate, and might be paraphrased "The event
of your watering it is a cause of the event of its future growing." (roda
zo'u lenu do jacysabji da cu rinka lenu da ba banro)

11. How can Lojban logical connectives be used in imperative
sentences? Logical connectives work properly only on complete
sentences, and of those, only those which actually assert something.

There is a special imperative pronoun ko. This is a second person
pronoun logically equivalent to do, the normal Lojban word for 'you',
but conveying an imperative sense. Thus, an imperative can be understood as commanding the listener to make true the assertion which
results when ko is replaced by do.

For example, ko sisti ('Stop!') is logically equivalent to do sisti ('you
stop'), and pragmatically may be understood as "Make 'do sisti' true!".
This allows logical connection to be used in imperatives without loss
of clarity or generality; the logical connection applies to the assertion
which is in effect embedded in the imperative.

So ko sisti .inaja mi ceclygau would seem to mean "Stop or I'll shoot",
but actually means "bring about a situation whereby, if you don't
stop, I'll shoot" —not quite the same thing. The sense of "stop or I'll

shoot" is properly conveyed by the phrase .i do bazi sisti .ijoinai mi ba ceclygau, "Either you will stop immediately, or I will shoot.".

A minor advantage of this style of imperative is that tensed imperatives like ko ba klama ('Come in-the-future!') become straightforward.

12. Since tense is optional in Lojban, how is a mixture of tensed and untensed sentences to be interpreted?

Lojban tense, like other incidental modifiers of a predication, tend to be contextually 'sticky'. Once specified in connected discourse, to whatever degree of precision seems appropriate, tense need not be respecified in each sentence. In narration, this assumption is modified to the extent that each sentence is assumed to refer to a slightly later time than the previous sentence, although with explicit tense markers it is possible to tell a story in reversed or scrambled time order. Therefore, each predication does have a tense, which is implicit if not necessarily explicit.

13. What theory underlies the choice of place structures?

Very little. Place structures are empirically derived, like the *gismu* list itself, and present a far more difficult problem; therefore, they were standardized rather late in the history of the project. There is no sufficiently complete and general case theory that allows the construction of *a priori* place structures for the large variety of predicates that exist in the real world.

The current place structures of Lojban represent a three-way compromise: fewer places are easier to learn; more places make for more concision (arguments not represented in the place structure may be added, but must be marked with appropriate case tags); the presence of an argument in the place structure makes a metaphysical claim that it is required for the predication to be meaningful.

This last point requires some explanation. For example, the predicate klama ('come, go') has five places: the actor, the destination, the origin, the route, and the means. Lojban therefore claims that anything not involving these five notions (whether specified in a particular sentence or not) is not an instance of klama. The predicate cliva ('leave') has the same places except for the destination; it is not necessary to be going anywhere in particular for cliva to hold. litru ('travel') has neither origin nor destination, merely, the actor, the route, and the means. The predicate cadzu ('walk'), involves a walker, a surface to walk on, and a means of walking (typically legs). One may walk without an origin or a destination (in circles, for instance); but walking in circles is not considered in Lojban to be 'going', as there is nowhere one is going to.

For describing the act of walking from somewhere to somewhere, the *tanru* cadzu klama or the corresponding *lujvo* dzukla would be appropriate. The *tanru* cadzu cliva and cadzu litru may be similarly analyzed.

14. How do borrowed words (*fu'ivla*) enter Lojban without compromising its stability and unambiguity?

There are four stages of borrowing in Lojban, as words become more and more modified (but shorter and easier to use). Stage 1 is the use of a foreign name quoted as it stands with the cmavo la'o. For example, me la'o ly. spaghetti .ly. is a predicate with the place structure "x_1 is a quantity of spaghetti." The foreign term is entirely unchanged. However, it requires five extra syllables and two pauses, and its pronunciation is unspecified.

Stage 2 involves changing the foreign name to a Lojbanized name: me la spagetis. This saves three syllables and one pause over Stage 1, and has a definite Lojban pronunciation. However, it is still awkward to use repeatedly.

Even so, one of these expedients is often quite sufficient when a word is needed quickly in conversation. This can make it easier to get by without a full command of the Lojban vocabulary—especially this early in the history of the language, when a wide range of vocabulary is yet to be devised.

Where a little more universality is desired, the word to be borrowed must be Lojbanized into one of several permitted forms. A *rafsi* is then attached to the beginning of the Lojbanized form, using an r or l to ensure that the resulting word doesn't fall apart. The result is a Stage 3 *fu'ivla* such as cidjrspageti, a true *brivla* (predicate word) rather than a phrase.

The *rafsi* used in a Stage 3 *fu'ivla* categorizes or limits its meaning; otherwise a word having several different jargon meanings in other languages would require the word-inventor to choose which single meaning should be assigned to the *fu'ivla*. (*fu'ivla*, like other *brivla*, are not permitted to have more than one definition.) Stage 3 borrowings are at present the most common kind of *fu'ivla*.

Finally, Stage 4 *fu'ivla* do not have any *rafsi* classifier, and are used where a *fu'ivla* has become so common or so important that it must be made as short as possible. The Stage 4 *fu'ivla* for 'spaghetti' is spageti; however, most Stage 4 words require a much greater distortion of the original form of the word. Stage 4 *fu'ivla* have to pass several careful morphological tests to eliminate confusion with existing words and phrases, and cannot easily be devised during conversation.

15. The Lojban phonological system is hard to use for English-speakers (to say nothing of Japanese-speakers), due to the large numbers of consonant clusters. How can a language be culturally neutral when it is difficult to pronounce?

Lojban phonology is carefully restricted. There are only 4 falling and 10 rising diphthongs, and the rising diphthongs are used only in names and in paralinguistic grunts representing emotions. All 25 possible vowel combinations are used, but they are separated by a voiceless vocalic glide written with an apostrophe, thus preventing diphthongization. English-speakers think of this glide as /h/, but even speakers of languages like French, which has no /h/, can manage this sound intervocalically.

Consonant clusters are carefully controlled as well. Only 48 selected clusters are permitted initially; some of these, such as ml and mr, do not appear in English, but are still possible to English-speakers with a bit of practice. Medial consonant clusters are also restricted, to prevent mixed voiced–unvoiced clusters, and other hard-to-handle combinations. The Lojban sound /y/, IPA [ə], is used to separate 'bad' medial clusters wherever the morphology rules would otherwise produce them.

The difficulties with the variety of permitted initial sounds are not as great as one might think. Initial consonant clusters occur only in content words (predicates) and names. These words seldom are spoken in isolation; rather, they are expressed in a speech stream with a rhythmic stress pattern, typically preceded by words that end with a vowel. The unambiguous morphology allows the words to be broken apart even if run together at a very high speech rate. Meanwhile, though, the final vowel of the preceding word serves to buffer the cluster, allowing it to be pronounced as a much easier medial cluster. Thus le mlatu ('the cat'), while officially pronounced /le,mla,tu/, can be pronounced as the easier /lem,la,tu/ with no confusion to the listener.

In addition, the buffering sound, IPA [ɪ] (the *i* of English *bit*), is explicitly reserved for insertion at any point into a Lojban word where the speaker requires it for ease of pronunciation. The word mlatu may be pronounced /mɪlatu/ by those who cannot manage ml, and nothing else need be changed. This sound is 'stripped' by the listener before any further linguistic processing is done.

16. Lojban words resemble their English cognates, but unsystematically so. Does this really aid learning, or does it make learning more difficult?

Lojban words only faintly resemble their English cognates. Most Lojban words are fairly equal mixtures of English and Chinese, with lesser influences from Spanish, Hindi, Russian, and Arabic.

There is no proven claim that the Lojban word-making algorithm has any meaningful correlation with learnability of the words. Informal 'engineering tests' were conducted early in the Loglan Project, leading to the selection of the current algorithm, but these tests have never been documented or subjected to review. The Logical Language Group has proposed formal tests of the algorithm, and has instrumented its vocabulary teaching software to allow data to be gathered that can confirm or refute this hypothesis. Gathering this data may incidentally provide insights into the vocabulary learning process, enabling Lojban to serve as a test bed for research in second language acquisition.

In any event, the word-making algorithm used for Lojban has the clear benefit of ensuring that phonemes occur in the language in rough proportion to their occurrence in the source natural languages, and in patterns and orders similar to those in the source languages. (Thus the first syllable of Lojban *gismu* most frequently ends in /n/, reflecting the high frequency of syllable-ending /n/ in Chinese.) The result is a language that is much more pleasant-sounding than, for example, randomly chosen phoneme strings, while having at least some claim to being free of the European cultural bias found in the roots of most other constructed languages.

17. What is the process by which the *gismu* were devised? What are some examples of the process and its results?

An appropriate term was chosen from each of the six languages used in the process: Chinese, English, Hindi, Spanish, Russian, Arabic. (Natural language forms below are given in this order, labeled by single letters.) In some cases, two different terms from one or another language were used, to see which would have the higher score. The terms were then converted to Lojban phonology, with the affricates reduced to their corresponding fricatives, to avoid a false match between the stop segment of a source-language affricate and a Lojban stop. Morphological affixes were removed, also to avoid false matches.

To score a candidate *gismu*, it was compared with each of the six source-language words to produce six raw scores. The raw score for a particular source word is roughly the number of letters it has in common (in the same order) with the candidate *gismu*. (If there are two or fewer letters in common, special rules apply.) The raw score was then divided by the length of the source-language word, and multiplied by a weight reflecting the relative number of speakers of the source language at the time the candidate *gismu* was devised. The sum of the six adjusted scores is the final score for that candidate *gismu*, typically expressed as a percentage.

For example, the candidate mamta for 'mother' was built from the following six source words, in Lojbanized form: C *ma*, E *mam*, H *mata*, S *mam*, R *mat*, A *am*. (The English forms are based on American English pronunciation and lexis.) The raw scores are 2, 3, 4, 3, 3, and 2 respectively, leading to a final score of 100%. Given the metrics of Lojban design, this word cannot be improved on!

At the other end of the spectrum is ciblu, the Lojban *gismu* for 'blood'. The source words here were C *ciue*, E *blad*, H *rakt*, S *sangr*, R *krof*, A *dam*. The raw scores are 3, 2, 0, 0, 0, 0 respectively; the adjusted scores are 0.27, 0.105, 0, 0, 0, 0; and the final score is 37.5%. This is quite low, since it reflects only the Chinese and English sources, but was still superior to all other possibilities devised.

The *gismu* cukta, meaning 'book', works out considerably better. Its sources are C *cu*, E *buk*, H *pustak*, S *libr*, R *knik*, A *kitab*, with raw scores of 2, 2, 3, 0, 0, 3 and a final score of 57.2%. Several different language families blended nicely to form this word.

Other *gismu* show similar patterns. prenu, for example, meaning 'person', is a mixture of Chinese *ren* and the 'person' root used in English, Spanish, and Russian. vanju, for 'wine' (Lojbanized as *vain*) matches well with every source language except Arabic, and even with French *vin* (which would Lojbanize as *van*), which is not a source language at all.

Finally, there is jmive, the *gismu* for '(a)live', which owes its form to a transcription error: the English source word was not Lojbanized to *laiv* but left as *live*. That this form has been retained in use shows that the etymology of Lojban *gismu* is now of secondary importance: retaining a stable vocabulary has become more important for the success of the language than fine-tuning its recognizability.

18. What is the standard word order of Lojban?

Lojban is only secondarily a 'word order' language at all. Primarily, it is a particle language. Using a standard word order allows many of the particles to be 'elided' (dropped) in common cases. However, even the standard unmarked word order is by no means fixed; the principal requirement is that at least one argument precede the predicate, but it is perfectly all right for all of the arguments to do so, leading to an SOV word order rather than the currently canonical SVO (subject–verb–object): the two orders are equally unmarked syntactically. VSO order is expressible using only one extra particle. In two-argument predicates, OSV, OVS, and VOS are also possible with only one particle, and various even more scrambled orders (when more than two-place predicates are involved) can also be achieved.

19. Lojban claims to be culturally neutral. But many of its conceptual distinctions, for example the color set, are clearly biased towards particular languages. There is a word for 'brown', which is a color not used in Chinese (although a word exists, it is rare); on the other hand, there is only one word for 'blue', although Russian-speakers convey the range of English 'blue' with two words. How can Lojban be prevented from splintering into dialects which differ in such points?

To some extent, such splitting is inevitable and already exists in natural languages. Some English-speakers may use the color term 'aqua' in their idiolect, whereas others lump that color with 'blue', and still others with 'green'. Understanding is still possible, perhaps with some effort. The Lojban community will have to work out such problems for itself; there are sufficient clarifying mechanisms to resolve differences in idiolect or style between individuals. The unambiguous syntax and other constraints defined in the language prescription should make such differences much more easily resolvable than, say, the differences between two dialects of English.

The prescriptive phase of Lojban is not intended to solve all problems (especially all semantic problems) but merely to provide enough structure to get a linguistic community started. After that, the language will be allowed to evolve naturally, and will probably creolize a bit in some cultures. Observing the creolization of such a highly prescribed constructed language will undoubtedly reveal much about the nature of the processes involved.

20. Lojban is supposed to be intended as a test of the Sapir–Whorf hypothesis in its negative form: "structural features of language make a difference in our awareness of the relations between ideas." Is this simply another way of saying "Distinctions are more likely to be noticed if structurally marked"? If so, this is trivially true.

A better paraphrase might be "Unmarked features are more likely to be used, and therefore will tend to constitute the backgrounded features of the language". By making the unmarked features those which are most unlike natural-language features, a new set of thought habits will be created (if Sapir–Whorf is true) which will be

measurably different from that of non–Lojban-speakers. If Sapir–
Whorf is false, which is the null hypothesis for Lojban purposes, no
such distinctions in thought habits will be detectable.

Further elaboration of Loglan/Lojban Project thinking about Sapir–
Whorf has led to an alternate formulation: "The constraints imposed
by structural features of language impose corresponding constraints
on thought patterns." In attempting to achieve cultural neutrality,
Lojban has been designed to minimize many structural constraints
found in natural languages (such as word order, and the structural
distinctions between noun, verb, and adjective). If Sapir–Whorf is
true, this should result in measurable broadening in thought patterns
(which may be manifested as increased creativity or ability to see
relationships between superficially unrelated concepts). Again, the
null hypothesis is that no measurable distinction will exist.

**21. How can 'ease of thought' be measured? Measuring facility with
predicate logic may not be enough to establish 'ease of thought'.**
Perhaps not. However, the Sapir–Whorf hypothesis may be confirmed
if experiments show that Lojban-speakers have a greater facility with
predicate logic than non–Lojban-speakers. That would indicate that
(natural) language limits thought in ways that Lojban-speakers can
bypass. This form of test is admittedly not free of its own difficulties,
which have been discussed elsewhere.

**22. What scientific and linguistic interest can Lojban possibly have,
since it is entirely a product of conscious design? Its study will only
reveal what its designers already put in the language—which surely
tells us little about language as it actually occurs among humans.**
Any language is a highly complex system—even an artificial
language, as long as it is non-trivial. (This certainly holds true for
Lojban!) In such a system, the interaction of the design features
displays properties that are more than the sum of its parts. For
example it is possible that all language is merely a system comprised
of a bunch of neurons releasing neurotransmitters. Biochemistry may
eventually devise a complete explanation for the neuronic process
(including its genetic components), and we may then say we "know

the design principles of the system." But we won't know the system, because the complexity of those neuronic interactions is so great that knowing the pieces does not give a total understanding of the system. This indeed may be what defines the concept of 'system'.

Knowing all the prescribed rules of an artificial language does not tell you how that artificial language is used communicatively. Consider this question: Given multiple ways of communicating the same idea, do users of the language choose particular forms over others, and why? This is similar to a question commonly asked about natural languages.

However, a simpler system, which can be understood more fully, may serve as an excellent model for a less well understood, more complex system. Thus the simpler system could be examined for parallels to hypotheses about the more complex system. Examination of the simpler system may suggest properties to look for in the more complex system, or it may even suggest hypotheses that can be tested in the more complex system. Constructing simplified models is after all how much of science—including a good deal of linguistics—is conducted.

A hot topic in parts of the Lojban community is whether the language has, or should have, an underlying semantic theory. If one exists, it is certainly not as developed or prescribed as the syntactic design and theory of the language. Eliminating syntactic ambiguity, however, does allow a more direct examination of semantic ambiguities, including the properties of modification and restriction, resolution of anaphora, and identification of ellipses. Any semantic theories proposed for natural language can be looked at in terms of semantic usage in the simpler Lojban system.

As a model of a natural language, it seems likely that any theory that is *not* true of Lojban is at the very least doubtful with regard to natural language, which would allow partial verification of such theories. If the theory is demonstrably true of natural language, then you have found evidence that Lojban is in some way unnatural. You would then need to explain which of the (fully-known) design features of Lojban causes this unnaturalness. Given the counter-example of Lojban, that design feature is not a feature of natural languages; this would demonstrate something about natural language by studying an artificial one.

As another example, pragmatic effects can be more easily recognized in the simpler Lojban system, and can be clearly identified as pragmatic. Thus, insights about pragmatic effects may be more visible in Lojban—and those insights would then be tested in natural languages.

23. Why is Lojban a useful testbed for experimental linguistics? What are some plausible experiments that could be done using Lojban?

As just discussed, a simple system is easier to perform experiments on than a more complex system. There are fewer variables, and if the system is 'designed', some things that are uncontrolled variables in complex systems are in effect tuneable constants in the simple, carefully-designed system. You can then rerun the experiment with minor changes to explore the effects of those variables.

Experimental linguistics of this kind is virtually unthinkable using natural languages. The Sapir–Whorf hypothesis is not really testable, since we can't control any pertinent variables in natural language, and we don't know what features of a language might be decisive in a culture. Sapir–Whorf may be more testable when you can reduce or even control the variables with a language like Lojban.

Lojban is a predicate language, with no distinct nouns, verbs, or adjectives. What are the linguistic (communicative) properties of such a system? The answer has been partially explored through symbolic logic. But do people, when thinking linguistically, mimic in any way the processes of formal logic? What effects would a formal-logic–based language have on those linguistic thinking processes? Is the resulting language susceptible to the same analysis as natural language, in terms of the various formal systems that have been developed by linguists over the past few decades?

Computational natural language processing usually involves converting natural language to some kind of predicate form, from which deductions can be made; so the usefulness of predicate logic as a tool for such analysis is already accepted. But how does one identify the logical deductions that a human being makes from a natural language statement? By thinking in Lojban, one is already thinking using predicate logic structures, so that the deduction process is much plainer.

If Lojban is shown by experiment to have the systemic properties of a natural language, and is easier to implement in computational linguistics research problems, it serves as a tool to bridge those two disciplines, leading to more rapid and effective natural language processing. But only if it is tried. Even if it proves less than ideal, the study of natural language using computational linguistic techniques and a Lojban-based tool can be instructive in ways not accessible using any natural language.

Lojban could also be used to study language acquisition. Take even a few children during the critical period of language learning and teach them this artificial language (at the same time as they learn their traditional language). Do they become truly bilingual? If they are as fluently communicative in the artificial language as they are in their natural language, then the artificial language is a suitable model of language; it becomes as real a language as any other. In that case, *any* theory of language that cannot encompass the features of the artificial language is inadequate. You could perform a series of experiments with ever more exotic artificial languages (obviously you would need new speakers for each test). Sooner or later, either the model breaks, and the artificial language is no longer acquirable by children or communicative as a language; or the theory breaks, and you've learned where to look for improvements in the theory.

With only natural languages, you have to devise theories based on the available data, and then look in other natural languages for confirmation or refutation. But this isn't the optimal kind of experimentation, because you really cannot plan the experiment or control the variables. (The other language may have the same apparent feature through a totally different process that you won't recognize, because you aren't looking for it.)

Lojban has a feature that is designed to explore a less-understood aspect of language—the direct expression of emotion. Lojban allows expressive communication of emotions in words without suprasegmental features such as intonation. This is presumably unlike all natural languages, though not entirely, as many languages have a limited set of indicators of attitude in the form of interjections. Can human beings manipulate the symbols of emotion, in the same way they manipulate the comparable symbols of non-emotional expression? There is a whole range of experimental questions raised by this design element, probably the most 'unnatural' element of Lojban's design.

A language like Lojban is an ideal test bed for experimentation, because it is flexible; you can evolve slightly different versions of the language very easily by simply changing some features. Delete a particular construct from the prescription, and do not teach it to a child. Does the child develop that construct anyway, by analogy to other known languages, or does the child successfully adapt to whatever other processes you've designed into the language instead of the omitted construct? Investigating questions like these through Lojban can help us significantly advance our understanding of language.

24. How is Lojban useful as a tool of linguistic analysis?
Here is an example, based on the 1991 Scientific American Library book *The Science of Words* (George A. Miller, Scientific American Library Series, New York: W H Freeman, 1996).

Miller notes that Nootka (a Pacific Northwest language) has the single word *inikwihl'minik'isit* meaning the equivalent of the entire English sentence "Several small fires were burning in the house." Here is a Lojban sentence closely paralleling the English:

so'i cmalu fagri	puca'o	jelca	ne'i	le zdani
Many small fires	were-then	burning	within	the house

But here is the sentence as a single word (though not with the same structure as Nootka):

zdane'ikemcmafagyso'ikemprununjelca

house-inside-type-of-small-fire-many-type-of-previous-burning

In fact, according to Miller the Nootka word breaks down as:

inikw	*-ihl*	*-'minih*	*-'is*	*-'it*
fire/burn	in-the-house	plural	diminutive	past-tense

This order is also readily expressible in Lojban:

> fagykemyzdanerso'icmapru
> fire-type-of-house-inside-many-small-past-event

In either case, the Lojban more accurately tracks the semantics of the Nootka, demonstrating the inadequacy of the English. The Nootka word as broken down did not require two separate semantic elements for 'fire' and 'burn' as did the English version, and the English translation used the more complicated tense 'were-burning' instead of the simpler, and presumably more accurate 'burned'. It is clear that in translating the word-sentence into English, considerable vagueness is introduced.

Lojban cannot, of course, express everything in the natural form of any language whatsoever. Lojban has a less-marked syntactic word order, and expressing other orders requires marking particles that would not be found in the source language. Thus there is a tradeoff between precise semantic and syntactic representations.

Still, this example suggests that, as a predicate language, Lojban is a much more effective tool at studying both the forms and semantics of other languages than is English, which has its own cultural, syntactic and semantic complexities to complicate the analysis. This is especially true for analysis by non-native English speaking linguists—if there is any place where there is a justification for an international, culturally minimalist language, it is when linguists from different native language backgrounds try to perform and communicate their linguistic analyses.

25. What sociolinguistic applications would Lojban have?

A language that begins with a highly detailed prescription and then is allowed to drift naturally is an ideal test bed for examining the processes of language change. In the case of an artificial language like Lojban, as the speaking community in each culture grows, you can observe how the language changes in contact with the speakers' native languages. Because of the speed of learning, artificial languages should tend to show effects more quickly (by being mastered to a communicative level more quickly). Anecdotal evidence about Esperanto supports this idea.

Does this mean that the conclusions are completely replicable to natural language evolutionary processes? Obviously not. But again, we are performing experiments with a model, somewhat idealized, of a natural language. Unlike a purely theoretical model (as all linguistic theories must inherently be), Lojban is a model that can be experimented with using live speakers. Provided that we understand the model as it evolves, that understanding approximates an understanding of natural language more closely as time goes on.

Furthermore, most numerically and sociologically important languages have some degree, more or less, of prescription. Indeed, some natural languages, such as modern Hebrew, formal Swahili, Mandarin Chinese, and modern standard Arabic, in certain ways resemble artificial languages, though they are regarded with more interest by linguists. A predominantly prescribed language would seem an especially effective tool for studying the effects of prescription on language development and use.

Such studies may aid in first-language education as well as second-language acquisition. They may also aid in analyzing the development of different registers (usages based on social class and situation) of a single language: such registers often arise partly as reactions to prescriptive environments that constrain language use.

None of these scientific applications of Lojban inherently requires a large fluent body of speakers, or any solely-native speaker of that tongue. If any of the less scientific applications of Lojban provide it with a speaker base, the nature of Lojban's usefulness as a model will change. New applications, not really predictable as yet, will turn up, aided by our doubtless increased understanding of language. But the model of language constituted by Lojban, even if well understood, no longer is as simple; and new logical languages and other experimental linguistic tools will need to be developed to take the next step.

III. Lojban Sample Texts

lojbo mupli bo seltcidu

Note: In the glosses, the following conventions apply:

( )	*sumti*
« »	*selbri*
[ ]	*bridi*
< >	abstraction/relativisation
{ }	grouping
boxed cell	semantic role of *sumti*

For instance:

.i $[_1(_2$dei$)_2$

'.'   this utterance   [is, does]

> *lisri$_1$ (story(ies))*

«$_3$lisri»$_3$ ($_4$le   <$_5$nu

being story(ies)   the   event(s) of

> *lisri$_2$ (plot)*

$[_6$«$_7$cpare»$_7$ ($_8$lo   cmana$)_8]_6$>$_5)_4]_1$

climb-ing   any/some   mountain(s)

> *cpare$_2$ (climbing surface(s))*

This indicates that **dei** is the first *sumti* of the *selbri* lisri (*lisri$_1$*); lenu cpare... is the second *sumti* of lisri (*lisri$_1$*); and cmana is the second *sumti* of the *selbri* cpare (*cpare$_2$*). Furthermore: **dei**, le nu cpare lo cmana, and cmana are *sumti*; lisri and cpare are *selbri*; nu cpare lo cmanais an abstraction; and the sentence contains two clauses: cpare lo cmana, and dei lisri le nu cpare lo cmana.

Chapter 5. bradi je bandu

By Arnt Richard Johansen (Norway), early 1999; Published at
Johansen's homepage, http://people.fix.no/arj/lojban/bradi-
je-bandu.html.

bi'u pa finti co jmive je prami
cu zutse co fengu gi'e pilno le skami
i darlu co darsi sai ne'i le zdani
i za'a le zekri lei turni cu xrani

i pa jdaralju co prami je krici
cu dunku bo catlu te farna le vrici
i malsi co krasi lo panpi bo stura
i turni co terpa lo nu se malxlura

i bi'u pa nanmu co krici je tavla
cu ca ve'u jgira bo cusku lo bravla
i misno bo sazri le slabu ke cradi
i ti'e le nanmu le jecta cu bradi

i uusai le bandu cu na'e se bandu
i za'a se jalge le nu mrocoldandu
i uosai le turni cu jmaji co salci
i sisti co zasti fa le remna co kalci

Enemies and defenders

There's an author, living and loving,
sitting angrily down in front of his computer.
He argues daringly within the house.
I see that the crime injures the rulers.

A priest, loving and believing,
is looking with anguish in various directions.
Temple which is a source for the structures of peace.
Government which is afraid of being fooled.

There's a man, believing and talking,
widely, proudly saying big words.
He is the famous operator of the familiar radio.
I hear that the man is an enemy of the state.

Unfortunately, the defenders were not defended.
I see that it results in death by hanging.
At last, the rulers can gather and celebrate.
The human waste is no longer here.

Gloss

bi'u	[₁(₂pa	{₃finti	co
{new information...}	1	create-r(s)	of-type

zutse₁ (sit-ter(s)), pilno₁ (use-r(s))

{₄jmive	je	prami}₄}₃)₂
live-r(s)	and	love-r(s)

cu	«₅{₆zutse	co	fengu}₆»₅
is/does	sit-ting	of-type	being angry

gi'e	«₇pilno»₇	(₈le	skami)₈]₁
and	us-ing	the	computer(s)

pilno₂ (tool(s))

.i	[₁«₂{₃darlu	co	darsi}₃»₂
'.'	argu-ing	of-type	dar-ing

sai	(₄ne'i	le	zdani)₄]₁
{strong attitude...}	inside	the	house(s)

.i	za'a	[$_1$($_2$le	zekri)$_2$
' '	{I observe...}	the	crime(s)

$xrani_1$ *(injur-er(s))*

($_3$lei	turni)$_3$	cu	«$_4$xrani»$_4$]$_1$
between them the	govern-er(s)	is/does	injur-ing

$xrani_2$ *(injured thing(s))*

.i	[$_1$($_2$pa	{$_3$jdaralju
' '	1	religion-chief(s)

$farna_3$ *(being origin(s) of direction)*

co	{$_4$prami	je	krici}$_4$}$_3$)$_2$
of-type	love-r(s)	and	believe-r(s)

cu	«$_5${$_6${$_7$dunku	bo	catlu}$_7$
is/does	distressed		look-ing at [type-of]

te farna}$_6$»$_5$	($_8$le	vrici)$_8$]$_1$
being origin(s) of direction	the	miscellaneous thing(s)

$farna_2$ *(thing(s) found in direction)*

.i	[$_1$«$_2${$_3$malsi	co	krasi}$_3$»$_2$
' '	being church(es)	of-type	being origin(s)

($_4$lo	{$_5$panpi	bo	stura}$_5$)$_4$]$_1$
any/some	thing(s) at peace		structure(s)

$krasi_2$ *(object(s)/process(es) with origin)*

.i	[$_1$«$_2${$_3$turni	co	terpa}$_3$»$_2$
' '	govern-ing	of-type	being fearful

($_4$lo	<$_5$nu	[$_6$«$_7$se malxlura»$_7$]$_6$>$_5$)$_4$]$_1$
any/some	event(s) of	derogative form-ish–tempted thing(s)

terpa$_2$ (thing(s) causing fear)

.i	bi'u	[$_1$($_2$pa	{$_3$nanmu
'.'	{new information...}	1	man/men

cusku$_1$ (say-er(s))

co	{$_4$krici	je	tavla}$_4$}$_3$)$_2$
of-type	believe-r(s)	and	talk-er(s)

cu	«$_5$ca	ve'u	{$_6$jgira
is/does	now	big space interval	being proud

bo	cusku}$_6$»$_5$	($_7$lo	bravla)$_7$]$_1$
	say-ing	any/some	big word(s)

cusku$_2$ (said thing(s))

.i	[$_1$«$_2${$_3$misno	bo	sazri}$_3$»$_2$
'.'	being famous		operat-ing

($_4$le	{$_5$slabu	ke	cradi}$_5$)$_4$]$_1$
the	familiar	type-of	broadcast-er(s)

sazri$_2$ (operated thing(s))

.i	ti'e	[$_1$($_2$le	nanmu)$_2$
'.'	{I hear...}	the	man/men

bradi$_1$ (enemy(ies))

($_3$le	jecta)$_3$	cu	«$_4$bradi»$_4$]$_1$
the	polity(ies)	is/does	being enemy(ies)

bradi$_2$ (thing(s) with enemy)

.i	.uu sai	$[_1(_2$le	bandu$)_2$
'.'	{strong regret...}	the	defender(s)

bandu$_2$ *(defended thing(s))*

cu	«$_3${$_4$na'e	se bandu}$_4$»$_3]_1$
is/does	other-than	being defend-ed

.i	za'a	$[_1$«$_2$se jalge»$_2$
'.'	{I observe...}	caus-ing outcome

($_3$le	<$_4$nu	$[_5$«$_6$mrocoldandu»$_6]_5$>$_4)_3]_1$
the	event(s) of	dead–of-type–thing(s) suspended

jalge$_1$ *(outcome(s))*

.i	.uo sai	$[_1(_2$le	turni$)_2$
'.'	{strong completion...}	the	govern-er(s)

jmaji$_1$ *(thing(s) gather-ing)*

cu	«$_3${$_4$jmaji	co	salci}$_4$»$_3]_1$
is/does	gather-ing	of-type	celebrat-ing

.i	$[_1$«$_2${$_3$sisti	co	zasti}$_3$»$_2$
'.'	ceas-ing	of-type	exist-ing

($_4$fa	le	{$_5$remna	co	kalci}$_5)_4]_1$
	the	human(s)	of-type	excrement

zasti$_1$ *(exist-er(s))*

Chapter 6. ckape litru

By Jorge Llambias (Argentina); posted on Lojban electronic mailing list, May 1994.

i dei lisri le nu cpare lo cmana
i go'i le nu sisku le ka manci
le rirci xrula poi titla se panci
zi'e poi ia xabju le traji cpana

i ca le nu finti dei kei mi zgana
le nu le romoi gusni pe le vanci
sekai le ka lazni cu masno canci
i le nu mi ciska dei cu te ckana

i xu frili fa le nu mi le zdani
cu cliva bai le banli mukti i na
go'i i ju le te zukte cu trina

i le pluta cu nandu gi'e clani
i ca binxo le lerci i le tsani
cu manku i ai mi catlu lo skina

Dangerous Journey

This is a tale of climbing a mountain.
A tale of seeking the wonder
of rare flowers, smelling sweet
and (so I believe) to be found at the very peak.

While writing this, I observe
the last light of the evening
slowly vanishing with laziness.
I'm writing this on a bed.

Is it easy for me to leave
my home, compelled by the great motive? Not
so. Whether or not the goal is attractive.

The path is difficult and long.
It's getting late. The sky
is dark. I'm going to watch a movie.

Gloss

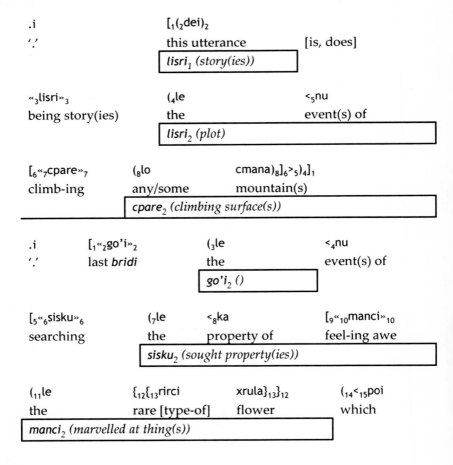

[$_{16}$"$_{17}${$_{18}$titla se panci}$_{18}$"$_{17}$]$_{16}$>$_{15}$ zi'e
sweet [type-of] emit-ting smell and

<$_{19}$poi .ia [$_{20}$"$_{21}$xabju"$_{21}$
which {belief...} dwell-ing

($_{22}$le {$_{23}$traji
the superlative [type-of]

---
xabju$_2$ (dwelling(s))
---

cpana}$_{23}$)$_{22}$]$_{20}$>$_{19}$)$_{14}$)$_{11}$]$_9$>$_8$)$_7$]$_5$>$_4$)$_3$]$_1$
on top of thing(s)

.i [$_1$($_2$ca le <$_3$nu [$_4$"$_5$finti"$_5$
'.' when the event(s) of creat-ing

($_6$dei)$_6$]$_4$ kei>$_3$)$_2$ ($_7$mi)$_7$
this utterance I

---
finti$_2$ (creation(s))   *zgana$_1$ (observe-r(s))*

"$_8$zgana"$_8$ ($_9$le <$_{10}$nu
[am, do] observ-ing the event(s) of
zgana$_2$ (observed thing(s))

[$_{11}$($_{12}$le {$_{13}${$_{14}$ro moi gusni}$_{14}$}$_{13}$
the is last among [type-of] light

---
canci$_1$ (vanish-er(s))

<$_{15}$pe ($_{16}$le vanci)$_{16}$>$_{15}$)$_{12}$ ($_{17}$se kai
associated with the evening(s) with property

le <$_{18}$ka [$_{19}$"$_{20}$lazni"$_{20}$]$_{19}$>$_{18}$)$_{17}$
the property of being lazy

cu	"$_{21}${$_{22}$masno	canci}$_{22}$"$_{21}$]$_{11}$)$_9$]$_1$
is/does	slow [type-of]	vanish-ing

.i	[$_1$($_2$le	<$_3$nu	[$_4$($_5$mi)$_5$
'.'	the	event(s) of	I
	ckana$_3$ (supported)		*ciska$_1$ (write-r(s))*

	"$_6$ciska"$_6$	($_7$dei)$_7$]$_4$>$_3$)$_2$
[am, do]	writ-ing	this utterance
		ciska$_2$ (written thing(s))

cu	te ckana"$_8$]$_1$
is/does	being supported by bed

.i	xu	[$_1$"$_2$frili"$_2$	($_3$fa	le
'.'	{yes/no?...}	being easy		the
			frili$_1$ (easy thing(s))	

<$_4$nu	[$_5$($_6$mi)$_6$	($_7$le	zdani)$_7$
event(s) of	I	the	home(s)
	cliva$_1$ (leave-r(s))	*cliva$_2$ (left thing(s))*	

cu	"$_8$cliva"$_8$	($_9$bai
is/does	leav-ing	compelled by

le	{$_{10}$banli	mukti}$_{10}$)$_9$]$_5$>$_4$)$_3$]$_1$
the	great [type-of]	motive(s)

.i	[$_1$"$_2${$_3$na	go'i}$_3$"$_2$]$_1$	.i	ju
'.'	not	last *bridi*	'.'	[whether or not]

[$_1$($_2$le	te zukte)$_2$	cu	"$_3$trina"$_3$]$_1$
the	purpose(s) of action	is/does	being attractive
trina$_1$ (attractive thing(s))			

.i   [₁(₂le   pluta)₂
'.'   the   route(s)

nandu₁ *(difficulty thing(s))*, clani₁ *(long thing(s))*

cu   «₃nandu»₃   gi'e   «₄clani»₄]₁
is/does   being difficulty and   being long

.i   [₁«₂ca   binxo»₂   (₃le   lerci)₃]₁
'.'   is/does   becom-ing   the   late thing(s)

binxo₂ *(result(s) of becoming)*

.i   [₁(₂le   tsani)₂   cu   «₃manku»₃]₁
'.'   the   sky(ies)   is/does   being dark

manku₁ *(dark thing(s))*

.i   .ai   [₁(₂mi)₂
'.'   {intent...}   I

catlu₁ *(look-er(s) at)*

           «₃catlu»₃   (₄lo   skina)₄]₁
[is, does]   looking-at   any/some   film(s)

catlu₂ *(looked at thing(s))*

Chapter 7. sera'a le cipnrkorvo .e le lorxu

Nick Nicholas (Australia); translated from Aesop from the Greek
(Fable 126). First published in *ju'i lobypli* 16, May 1992.

sera'a le cipnrkorvo .e le lorxu

.i lo cipnrkorvo noi ba'o kavbu lo rectu cu co'a zutse lo tricu
.i lo lorxu noi viska ra gi'e djica lenu cpacu le rectu
cu sanli gi'e zanru skicu le cipnrkorvo. ri lo xadbraxau je melbi
gi'eji'a bacru lesedu'u ge ra nu'o turni .ei lei cipni
gi leda'inu ra cu se voksa lo xamgu cu nibli lenu pu'i turni
.i le cipnrkorvo noi djica lenu jarco fi le lorxu
fe leka pu'i se voksa lo xamgu cu renro le rectu gi'e cladu krixa
.i le lorxu cu bajra gi'e bacru ba'o lenu kavbu le rectu kei
    lu doi cipnrkorvo noda
    fau leda'inu do se menli lo xamgu
    cu fanta lenu do turni roda li'u
ni'o le prenu noi bebna ku'o le se cusku cu pilno se xamgu

Crow and Fox

A crow, having snatched some meat, sat on a tree. And a fox seeing
him, and wishing to obtain the meat, stood and praised him as well-
proportioned and beautiful—also saying that he should indeed be
king of the birds, and that this would have happened, if he had a
[good] voice. And wishing to show her that he too had a voice, he
threw off the meat and shouted loudly. And having run to him and
snatched the meat, she said: "O Crow, if you had brains too, nothing
would be lacking for you to be king of everything."
    The word is opportune for a foolish man.

Gloss

[₁(₂sera'a	{₃{₄le	cipnkorvo
concerning	the	bird(s)-*Corvus*

.e	le	lorxu}₄}₃)₂]₁
and	the	fox(es)

.i	[₁(₂lo	{₃cipnrkorvo}₃	<₄noi
'.'	any/some	bird(s)-*Corvus*	, which...,

zutse₁ *(sit-ter(s))*

[₅«₆ba'o	kavbu»₆	(₇lo	rectu)₇]₅>₄)₂	cu
finished	captur-ing	any/some	meat	is/does

kavbu₂ *(captured thing(s))*

«₈co'a	zutse»₈	(₉lo	tricu)₉]₁
start to	sit-ting	any/some	tree(s)

zutse₂ *(sitting surface(s))*

.i	[₁(₂lo	{₃lorxu}₃	<₄noi	[₅«₆viska»₆
'.'	any/some	fox(es)	, which...,	see-ing

zutse₁ *(stand-er(s))*, **skicu₁** *(describe-r(s))*, **bacru₁** *(utter-er(s))*

(₇ra)₇		gi'e	«₈djica»₈
the former		and	desir-ing

viska₂ *(seen thing(s))*

(₉le	<₁₀nu	[₁₁«₁₂cpacu»₁₂
the	event(s) of	acquir-ing

djica₂ *(desired thing(s))*

(₁₃le	rectu)₁₃]₁₁>₁₀)₉]₅>₄)₂	cu	«₁₄sanli»₁₄
the	meat	is/does	stand-ing

cpacu₂ *(acquired thing(s))*

gi'e	«₁₅{₁₆zanru	skicu}₁₆»₁₅
and	approv-ing [type of]	describ-ing

$(_{17}$le	cipnrkorvo$)_{17}$	$(_{18}$ri$)_{18}$
the	bird(s)-*Corvus*	the latter

skicu*$_2$ *(described thing(s))	***skicu*$_3$ *(audience(s) for describing)***

$(_{19}$lo	$\{_{20}$xadbraxau		je	melbi$\}_{20})_{19}$
any/some	body-large–good thing(s)		and	beautiful thing(s)

skicu*$_4$ *(description(s))

gi'e	ji'a	«$_{21}$bacru»$_{21}$	$(_{22}$le	se <$_{23}$du'u
and	{in addition...}	utter-ing	the	fact expressed by

bacru*$_2$ *(uttered sound(s))

$[_{24}$ge	$[_{25}(_{26}$ra$)_{26}$		«$_{27}$nu'o
both	the former	[is, does]	can but has not

turni*$_1$ *(govern-er(s))

turni	.ei»$_{27}$	$(_{28}$lei	cipni$)_{28}]_{25}$
govern	{obligation...}	between them the	bird(s)

turni*$_2$ *(governed thing(s))

gi	$[_{29}(_{30}$le	da'i
and	the	{supposing...}

nibli*$_1$ *(logically necessitating thing(s))

<$_{31}$nu	$[_{32}(_{33}$ra$)_{33}$	cu
event(s) of	the former	is/does

voksa*$_2$ *(thing(s) having voice)

«$_{34}$se voksa»$_{34}$	$(_{35}$lo	xamgu$)_{35}]_{32}$>$_{31})_{30}$
having voice	any/some	good thing(s)

voksa*$_1$ *(voice sound(s))

cu $\quad\quad\quad\quad$ «$_{36}$nibli»$_{36}$
is/does $\quad\quad\quad\quad$ logically necessitating

($_{37}$le $\quad\quad\quad$ <$_{38}$nu $\quad\quad\quad\quad\quad\quad\quad$ [$_{39}$«$_{40}$pu'i
the $\quad\quad\quad\quad$ event(s) of $\quad\quad\quad\quad\quad$ can and be

nibli$_2$ (logically necessitated thing(s))

turni»$_{40}$]$_{39}$>$_{38}$)$_{38}$]$_{37}$]$_{29}$]$_{24}$>$_{23}$)$_{22}$]$_1$
govern-ing

.i $\quad\quad$ [$_1$($_2$le $\quad\quad$ {$_3$cipnrkorvo}$_3$ $\quad\quad\quad$ <$_4$noi
'.' $\quad\quad$ the $\quad\quad\quad$ bird(s)-*Corvus* $\quad\quad$, which...,

renro$_1$ (throw-er(s)), krixa$_1$ (yell-er(s))

[$_5$«$_6$djica»$_6$ $\quad\quad$ ($_7$le $\quad$ <$_8$nu $\quad\quad\quad$ [$_9$«$_{10}$jarco»$_{10}$
desir-ing $\quad\quad\quad$ the $\quad$ event(s) of $\quad\quad$ showing/display-ing

djica$_2$ (desired thing(s))

($_{11}$fi $\quad$ le $\quad\quad$ lorxu)$_{11}$ $\quad\quad\quad$ ($_{12}$fe $\quad$ le $\quad\quad$ <$_{13}$ka
$\quad\quad\quad$ the $\quad\quad$ fox(es) $\quad\quad\quad\quad\quad\quad$ the $\quad$ property of

jarco$_3$ (audience of display)	*jarco$_2$ (shown property(ies))*

[$_{14}$«$_{15}$pu'i $\quad\quad\quad\quad\quad\quad\quad\quad$ se voksa»$_{15}$
can and does $\quad\quad\quad\quad\quad\quad\quad\quad$ having voice

($_{16}$lo $\quad\quad\quad\quad$ xamgu)$_{16}$]$_{14}$>$_{13}$)$_{12}$]$_9$>$_8$)$_7$]$_5$>$_4$)$_2$
any/some $\quad\quad\quad\quad$ good thing(s)

xamgu$_1$ (voice sound(s))

cu $\quad\quad\quad\quad$ «$_{17}$renro»$_{17}$ $\quad\quad$ ($_{18}$le $\quad\quad\quad\quad$ rectu)$_{18}$
is/does $\quad\quad\quad\quad$ throw-ing $\quad\quad\quad$ the $\quad\quad\quad\quad$ meat

$\quad\quad\quad\quad\quad\quad\quad\quad\quad\quad\quad\quad\quad\quad\quad\quad$ *renro$_2$ (thrown thing(s))*

gi'e	«19{20cladu	krixa}20»19]1
and	loud [type-of]	yell-ing

.i	[1(2le	lorxu)2	cu
'.'	the	fox(es)	is/does

> bajra1 *(run-ner(s)),* bacru1 *(utter-er(s))*

«3bajra»3	gi'e	«4bacru»4	(5ba'o	le
run-ning	and	utter-ing	after	the

<6nu	[7«8kavbu»8	(9le	rectu)9]7	kei>6)5
event(s) of	capturing	the	meat	

> kavbu2 *(captured thing(s))*

(10lu	(11{12doi	cipnrkorvo}12)11
"	O!	bird(s)-*Corvus*

> bacru2 *(uttered sound(s))*

[13(14no	da)14	(15fau	le	da'i
0 (of)	X	in the event of	the	{supposing...}

> fanta2 *(prevent-er(s))*

<16nu	[17(18do)18	
event(s) of	you	[is, does]

> menli2 *(of body)*

«19se menli»19	(20lo	xamgu)20]17>16)15
being body(ies) with mind	any/some	good thing(s)

> menli1 *(mind(s))*

cu	«21fanta»21	(22le	<23nu
is/does	prevent-ing	the	event(s) of

> fanta2 *(prevented event(s))*

155

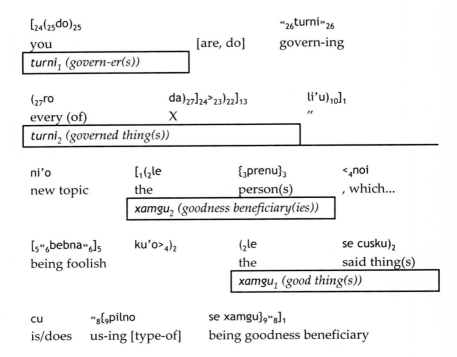

[24(25do)25   "26turni"26
you   [are, do]   govern-ing
turni1 (govern-er(s))

(27ro   da)27]24>23)22]13   li'u)10]1
every (of)   X   "
turni2 (governed thing(s))

ni'o   [1(2le   {3prenu}3   <4noi
new topic   the   person(s)   , which...
xamgu2 (goodness beneficiary(ies))

[5"6bebna"6]5   ku'o>4)2   (2le   se cusku)2
being foolish   the   said thing(s)
xamgu1 (good thing(s))

cu   "8{9pilno   se xamgu}9"8]1
is/does   us-ing [type-of]   being goodness beneficiary

Chapter 8. Attitudinal

By Nora Tansky LeChevalier (USA); printed in *The Complete Lojban Language* (John W. Cowan, Fairfax, VA: Logical Language Group, 1997), Chapter 13.15.

la rik. .e la .alis. nerkla le kafybarja
Rick and Alice in-go to-the coffee-bar.
Rick and Alice go into the coffee bar.

.i sei la rik. cusku se'u
   ta'a ro zvati be ti
   mi baza speni ti .iu
[Comment] Rick says, [end-comment]
   [Interrupt] all at this-place,
   I [future] [medium] am-spouse-to this-one [love].
Rick said, "Sorry to break in, everybody. Pretty soon I'm getting married to my love here."

.i sei la djordj. cusku se'u
   a'o ko gleki doi ma
[Comment] George says, [end-comment]
[Hope] [You-imperative] are-happy, O [who?].
George said, "I hope you'll be happy, um, ...?"

.i sei la pam. cusku se'u
   pe'u .alis.
   xu mi ba terfriti lenu zvati le nunspenybi'o
[Comment] Pam says,
   [Please] Alice, [end-comment]
   [Is it true?] I [future] receive-offer-of the event of being-present-at the event-of-spouse-becoming?
Pam said, "Please, Alice, am I going to be invited to the wedding?"

.i sei la mark. cusku se'u
   coi baza speni

.a'o le re do lifri le ka gleki
[*Comment*] *Mark says,* [*end-comment*]
   [*Greetings*] [*future*] [*medium*] *spouse(s),*
   [*Hope*] *the two of-you experience the-property-of being-happy*
Mark said, "Hello, spouses-to-be. I hope both of you will be very happy."

.i sei la rik. cusku se'u
  mi'e .rik. doi terpreti
[*Comment*] *Rick says,* [*end-comment*]
   [*I am*] *Rick, O questioners.*
Rick said, "My name is Rick, for those of you who want to know."

.i sei la .alis. cusku se'u
  nu'e .pam. .o'ero'i
  do ba zvati
[*Comment*] *Alice says,* [*end-comment*]
   [*Promise-to*] *Pam,* [*closeness*] [*emotional*]
   you [*future*] *are-at.*
Alice said, "I promise you'll be there, Pam honey."

.i sei la fred. cusku se'u
  .uinaicairo'i
  mi ji'a prami la .alis.
  fe'o .rik.
[*Comment*] *Fred says,* [*end-comment*]
   [*Happy*] [*not*] [*emphatic*] [*emotional*]
   I [*additionally*] *love Alice.*
   [*Over and out to*] *Rick.*
"I love Alice too," said Fred miserably. "Have a nice life, Rick."

.i la fred. cliva
Fred leaves.
And he left.

.i sei la rik. cusku se'u
  fi'i ro zvati
  ko pinxe pa ckafi fi'o pleji mi

[Comment] Rick says, [end-comment]
  [Welcome-to] all at-place,
  [You-imperative] drink one coffee with-payer me.
Rick said, raising his voice, "A cup of coffee for the house, on me."

.i sei la pam. cusku se'u
  be'e selfu
[Comment] Pam says, [end-comment]
  [Request to speak to] server.
Pam said, "Waiter!"

.i sei le selfu cu cusku se'u
  re'i
[Comment] The server says, [end-comment]
  [Ready to receive].
The waiter replied, "May I help you?"

.i sei la pam. cusku se'u
  .e'o ko selfu le traji xamgu ckafi le baza speni
  fi'o pleji mi
[Comment] Pam says, [end-comment]
  [Petition] [You-imperative] serve the (superlatively good) coffee to-the
[future] [medium] spouse
  with-payment me.
Pam said, "One Jamaica Blue for the lovebirds here, on my tab."

.i sei le selfu cu cusku se'u
  vi'o
[Comment] The server says, [end-comment]
  [Will comply].
"Gotcha", said the waiter.

.i sei la rik. cusku se'u
  ki'e .pam.
[Comment] Rick says, [end-comment]
  [Thanks O] Pam.
"Thanks, Pam", said Rick.

.i sei la pam. cusku se'u
  je'e
[Comment] *Pam says, [end-comment]*
  [Acknowledge].
"Sure", said Pam.

.i sei la djan. cusku se'u
  .y. mi .y. mutce spopa .y.
  le nu le speni si .y.
  ba speni .y. .y.
  su .yyyyyy. mu'o
[Comment] *John says, [end-comment]*
  [Uh] I [uh] very [hope (in Institute Loglan)] [uh]
  the event-of the spouse [erase] [uh]
  [future] spouse [uh] [uh]
  [erase all] [uh] [over]
John said, "I, er, very hoffen, uh, marriage, upcoming marriage, ...
Oh, forget it. Er, later."

.i sei la djordj. cusku se'u
  ke'o .djan. zo'o
[Comment] *George says, [end-comment]*
  [Repeat O] John [humor].
"How's that again, John?" said George.

.i sei la pam. cusku se'u
  ju'i .djordj.
  .e'unai le kabri bazi farlu
[Comment] *Pam says, [end-comment]*
  [Attention] George,
  [Warning] the cup [future] [short] falls
"George, watch out!" said Pam. "The cup's falling!"

.i le kabri cu je'a farlu
The cup indeed falls.
The cup fell.

.i sei la djan. cusku se'u
   .e'o doi djordj. zo'o rapygau
[Comment] John says, [end-comment]
   [Petition] O George [humor] repeat-cause.
John said, "Try that again, George!"

.i sei la djordj. cusku se'u
   co'o ro zvati pe secau la djan. ga'i
[Comment] George says, [end-comment]
   [Partings] all at-place without John [superiority]
"Goodbye to all of you," said George sneeringly, "except John."

.i la djordj. cliva
George leaves.
George left.

Appendix A. Complete Pronunciation Guide

mulno ke bacru tadji velciski

The pronunciation guide that appeared in the Overview is intended for speakers of North American English. This more complete pronunciation guide uses the International Phonetic Alphabet, and comparison with the other five source languages of Lojban, in order to be useful outside North America.

Rather than concentrate on precise phonetic targets, Lojban phonemes have a range of allowed pronunciations, although there are preferred variants (given first in the IPA chart below.) The intent is to allow speakers to be understood unambiguously, rather than to devise a specific Lojban 'accent'. Where no word has been given to illustrate the pronunciation of a Lojban phoneme in a language, no phoneme in that language is close enough to serve as an equivalent.

International Phonetic Alphabet

a	[a] ([ɑ]): an open vowel
b	[b]: a voiced bilabial stop
c	[ʃ] ([ʂ]): an unvoiced coronal sibilant
d	[d]: a voiced dental/alveolar stop
e	[ɛ] ([e]): a front mid vowel
f	[f] ([ɸ]): an unvoiced labial fricative
g	[g]: a voiced velar stop
i	[i]: a front close vowel
j	[ʒ] ([ʐ]): a voiced coronal sibilant
k	[k]: an unvoiced velar stop
l	[l] ([l̩]): a voiced lateral approximant (may be syllabic)
m	[m] ([m̩]): a voiced labial nasal (may be syllabic)
n	[n] ([n̩, ŋ, ɲ]): a voiced dental, alveolar or velar nasal (may be syllabic)

o	[o] ([ɔ]): a back mid vowel
p	[p]: an unvoiced bilabial stop
r	[r] ([ɹ, ɾ, ʀ, ɽ, ɻ, ɿ, ʁ]): a rhotic sound
s	[s]; an unvoiced alveolar sibilant
t	[t]: an unvoiced dental/alveolar stop
u	[u]: a back close vowel
v	[v] ([β]): a voiced labial fricative
x	[x]: an unvoiced velar fricative
y	[ə]; a central mid vowel
z	[z]: a voiced alveolar sibilant
'	[h] ([θ]): an unvoiced glottal spirant
.	[ʔ]: a glottal stop or a pause
ai	[aj] ([ɑj])
au	[aw] ([ɑw])
ei	[ɛj] ([ej])
oi	[oj] ([ɔj])
ia	[ja] ([jɑ])
ie	[jɛ] ([je])
ii	[ji]
io	[jo] ([jɔ])
iu	[ju]
ua	[wa] ([wɑ])
ue	[wɛ] ([we])
ui	[wi]
uo	[wo] ([wɔ])
uu	[wu]

Arabic

a	qāl قال , hāḏā هاذا
b	buṭrus بطروس , binzīn بــنزين
c	šatt شط , šaḥṣ شخص
d	diyār ديار , dar' درء
e	bel بَــلْ, merkebun مَــرْكَبّ

f	*f*arq فرق , *f*akka فك
g	Egyptian pronunciation of *g*amīla جميلة , *g*iddan جدا
i	bī*i*a بــيـع , s*ī*r ســين
j	Does not exist in Arabic, but dj corresponds to *j*amīla جميلة , *j*iddan جدا
k	*k*at̲ira كــثيرة , *k*ull كل
l	*l*aṭofa لطف , *l*ā لا
m	*m*atār مطار, *m*arḥaba مرحبا
n	*n*aṣr نصر , *n*aṣaḥanī نصــحني
o	m*o*tun مَوُتّ , s*o*tna صَـــوُتنّ
p	
r	*r*usūm رسوم , *r*aḥīṣ رخيص
s	*s*iḥrun سحر , *s*ayyāra ســيارة
t	*t*askun تسـكن, *t*asbaḥ تســبح
u	s*ū*q سوق , q*ū*wila قوول
v	
x	*x̲*ala'a خلع , *x̲*aṣṣatan خاصة
y	muḥammad مُــحَمَدْ, m*i*sāfir مِســـافِرْ
z	*z*awājī زواجي, *Z*eid زيد
'	bi*h*i به , la*h*u له
.	mas-'alatun مسالة , al-qur'ān القرآن
ai	ṣ*ai*fun صَـــيْفّ, tarḍ*ai*na تَـــرْضَــيْنَ
au	x̲*au*fun خَـوْفّ
ei	qub*ei*la قُــبَــيْلَ, bun*ei*yun بُــنَــيٌّ
oi	
ia	miṣr*iyy*āt مصريات , sayyāra ســيارة
ie	y*e*dai يَـدَيْ
ii	
io	
iu	y*ū*qifu يِـوقف, y*ū*bisu يــوبس

ua	ṭuwāla طوال, šaqrāwāt شقراوات
ue	
ui	suwīdiyyāt ســـويديات
uo	
uu	wufūd وُفُـــوْد

Chinese (Putonghua/Mandarin)

a	mǎshang 馬上/ 马上
b	búbiàn 不便/ 不便, bīngbáo 冰雹/ 冰雹
c	shāwěi 搰尾/ 搰尾, shān shang 山上/ 山上
d	Datong 大同/ 大同, dōngfāng 東方/ 东方, dǎdǎo 打倒/ 打倒
e	fēi 飛/ 飞
f	fēngshǔi 風水/ 风水, fei long wu feng 飛龍舞鳳/ 飞龙舞凤
g	gāoliáng 高粱/ 高粱, zāogāo 糟糕/ 糟糕
i	bīnglì 兵力/ 兵力
j	
k	kèrén 客人/ 客人, kāikǒu 開口/ 开口
l	Aolóng 奧龍/ 奥龙, lúnlíu 輪流/ 轮流
m	máfàn 麻煩/ 麻烦, míngmèi 明媚/ 明媚
n	Nanning 南寧/ 南宁, nénglì 能力/ 能力, nóngrén 農人/ 农人
o	duō 多/ 多, wǒ 我/ 我
p	pinyin 拼音/ 拼音, hépīng 和平/ 和平
r	rén 人/ 人, ráng 讓/ 让, értóng 兒童/ 儿童
s	sānjiǎo 三角/ 三角, sǎngménr 嗓悶兒/ 嗓闷儿
t	Tang 唐/ 唐, tèbié 特別/ 特别
u	daòlu 道路/ 道路, gōngfū 功夫/ 功夫, gǔwù 古物/ 古物
v	
x	hen hao 很好/ 很好
y	shénme 甚麼/ 什么, wǒ lái le 我來了/ 我来了
z	
,	
.	
ai	lái 來/ 来, báicái 白菜/ 白菜
au	lǎo 老/ 老, zāogāo 糟糕/ 糟糕

ei	F*ei*zhou 非洲/ 非洲, M*ei*guo 美國/ 美国, B*ei*jing 北京/ 北京
oi	fat ch*oi* in Cantonese (fā cài 發財/ 发财)
ia	Y*a*zhou 亞洲/ 亚洲, y*ā*zi 鴨子/ 鸭子, y*á*ngrén 洋人/ 洋人
ie	l*iè*fēng 烈風/ 烈风, m*iè*wáng 滅亡/ 灭亡
ii	Y*i*ngguo 英國/ 英国, y*ī* 一/ 一, y*ì*wén 譯文/ 译文
io	péng*yǒ*u 朋友/ 朋友, n*iú*ròu → n*you* 牛肉/ 牛肉
iu	y*ò*nggōng 用功/ 用功
ua	bāg*uà* 八卦/ 八卦
ue	wu + ye → we 五葉/ 五叶
ui	Pu-*yi* 溥儀/ 溥仪 (don't pronounce the y!)
uo	L*uo*ma 羅馬/ 罗马
uu	w*úbǐ* 無比/ 无比

Hindi & Urdu

a	*āg* आग اگ , *āp* आप اپ
b	*bandar* बंदर بـندر , *barf* बरफ़ برف
c	*śer* शेर شـیر, *śahar* शहर شهر
d	*dard* दरद درد , *das* दस دیش
e	*ek* एक ایـك, *ekānt* एकांत ایکانـر
f	*farś* फ़रश فـرش, *fasl* फ़सल فصـل (as in Urdu)
g	*garam* गरम گـرم, *gardan* गरदन گـردن
i	*īś* ईश ایش, *īkh* ईख ه ایـك
j	Does not exist in Hindi, but dj corresponds to *jab* जब جب, *jaldī* जलदी جلدی
k	*kab* कब کب, *kamal* कमल کمل
l	*laṛkī* लड़की لـڑکی, *lahar* लहर لهـر
m	*magar* मगर مگـر, *man* मन من
n	*nagar* नगर نگـر, *namak* नमक نـمك
o	*oṛnā* ओढ़ना اوڑهـنـا, *omṭh* ओठ اونـئه
p	*pakaṛ* पकड़ پکـڑ, *pacapan* पचपन پچـپن
r	*rāt* रात رات , *rāstā* रासता راسـته
s	*sab* सब سب, *samajh* समझ سـمجھ
t	*tab* तब تب, *tarah* तरह طـره
u	*ūpar* ऊपर اوپـر, *ūn* ऊन اون

v	*vah* वह ولہ , *vajah* वजह وجہ
x	*xabar* ख़बर حبر, *xatm* ख़तम حتم (as in Urdu)
y	*ab* अब اب , *agar* अगर اگر
z	*zarūr* ज़रूर ضرور, *zindā* ज़िंदा زنده (as in Urdu)
'	*kahīṁ* कहीं كهاں, *dehāt* देहात ديهات
.	
ai	*gāy* गाय گاي, *cāy* चाय چاي
au	
ei	
oi	
ia	*yā* या يا, *bāyāṁ* बायाँ باياں
ie	*ye* ये یے , *jyeṣṭh* ज्येष्ठ ژيستھ
ii	
io	*kyoṁ* क्यों كيوں, *prayoj* परयोज پريوج
iu	*yūn* यूं یوں, *yūropīya* यूरोपीय يوروپييہ
ua	*darvāza* दरवाज़ा دروازے , *itvār* इतवार اتوار
ue	*svet* संबेत سویت, *śveshṭ* श्रबेषट شویش
ui	*tasvīr* तसबीर تصویر, *svīkār* सबीकार سویکار
uo	
uu	

Russian

a	масса
b	быть
c	шар
d	дать
e	это
f	телефон
g	гора
i	число
j	женщина
k	кот
l	луна
m	мать
n	нос
o	том

p	запад
r	рубль
s	сосэд
t	тут
u	шум
v	вотум
x	хорошо
y	колокол
z	злой
'	
.	
ai	читай
au	
ei	действо
oi	Толстой
ia	я являю
ie	еврейский
ii	
io	узнаете
iu	уютную
ua	
ue	
ui	
uo	
uu	

Spanish

a	*ala*
b	*bote* (plosive, not fricative)
c	*show*
d	*dato* (plosive, not fricative)
e	*este*
f	*foto*
g	*gato* (plosive, not fricative)
i	*iris*
j	*lluvia* (some accents), *perro* (some accents)
k	*kilo*

l	*luna*
m	*mano*
n	*nube*
o	*oso*
p	*pato*
r	*pero, perro*
s	*sapo*
t	*tapa*
u	*uno*
v	*nieve*
x	*jaula*
y	
z	*Israel* (voiced)
'	*lejos* (some accents)
.	
ai	*aire*
au	*auto*
ei	*reino*
oi	*oigo*
ia	*piano*
ie	*piedra*
ii	*allí* (some accents)
io	*piojo*
iu	*ciudad*
ua	*cuatro*
ue	*puente*
ui	*ruido*
uo	*cuota*
uu	

Index

LaVergne, TN USA
07 March 2010
175225LV00003B/26/A